God's Wrath is
GOOD NEWS

H. Dave Derkson

GOD'S WRATH IS GOOD NEWS

Unless otherwise indicated, all scripture quotations are taken
from the New King James Version®. Copyright © 1982 by
Thomas Nelson, Inc. Used by permission. All rights reserved.
Scripture quotations marked NIV are taken from the Holy Bible,
New International Version. Copyright © 1973, 1978, 1984 International Bible Society. Used by permission of Zondervan Bible
Publishers. Scripture quotations marked AMP are taken from
the Amplified Bible, Copyright © 1954, 1958, 1962, 1964, 1965,
1987 by The Lockman Foundation. Used by permission.

ISBN-13: 978-1-77069-179-7

Printed in Canada.

Word Alive Press
131 Cordite Road, Winnipeg, MB R3W 1S1
www.wordalivepress.ca

Library and Archives Canada Cataloguing in Publication

Derkson, H. Dave (Harold David), 1940-
     God's wrath is good news / H. Dave Derkson.

Includes bibliographical references.
ISBN 978-1-77069-179-7

     1. God--Wrath. I. Title.

BT153.W7D47 2010   231'.4   C2010-907461-0

PREFACE

This book is about God's wrath, but it may not be what you expect. Many people think of God's wrath as his compelling desire to punish sinners. If you think that God has an overwhelming desire to punish you, you need to read this book. On the other hand, if you are religious and hold to the above definition of God's wrath, you may not want to read this book, because it will challenge your religious thinking! But if you have wrestled with questions about God's wrath, like I have, then this book is for you.

I began to question popular teachings concerning God's wrath some twenty-five years ago. A study of what the Bible said about God's anger became a personal quest for me. In my studies, I gave priority to the source—the Bible—from which theologians glean their respective teachings concerning God's character. I specifically questioned the religious presentation of God as a loving father, but at the same time a strict, avenging, authoritarian one who will punish all sinners.

According to the four Gospel writers—Matthew, Mark, Luke, and John—Jesus often referred to God as his father. I had some issues with God being portrayed as a father. My own father committed suicide when I was eleven years old. For some time after his funeral, I had nightmares of my dad being angry with me. Was God like my dad, and was he capable of unspeakable violence?

Some theologians present God as being capable of extreme violence while at the same time portraying him as a loving father. Yes, it's true that they portray God as a loving father who provides the people of the world with redemption from destruction and death. Yet some of those same theologians hold that at some point God will punish the sinners of this world. These theologians suggest that when that day comes, things will not be pleasant on this earth. Theologians who follow this train of thought seem to think that instilling a fear of God in people is the way to bring them to faith in God.

My studies brought me to a serendipitous realization: Jesus Christ became the personification of God's wrath against all sin, and every sinner. Jesus took upon himself the sins of the world and stood under condemnation in our place. That realization opened to me a door into new vistas about God, which resulted in the book you now hold in your hand.

I've come to understand the Bible as telling us that God loves people unconditionally! God has no intention of—nor does he desire or take pleasure in—punishing the human race. As you read, I trust you will come to know and understand God as a loving father, full of grace, mercy and truth. He is a father who wants and seeks to have a relationship with you. He desires to guide you through the maze of evil that exists in this world. He does not want you to be overcome by that evil, but instead wants you to overcome evil. He has destined you for greatness, and his desire is to be personally involved in every step of your journey to achieve greatness. God wants to keep you from making choices that are destructive to yourself and others. My prayer is that as you read you will come to know God as a father who truly loves you and has your best interests at heart.

FOREWORD

As an editor, I do a lot of reading. In the Christian market in particular, I find there are a lot of books filled with good information and solid advice as it pertains to helping Christians live out their faith. Many others offer powerful, real-world stories of triumph over adversity. Indeed, a great Christian book should be educational and instructive—but above all, it should inspire us to be better people, make wiser choices, and stimulate within ourselves a closer relationship with God.

Another fundamental ingredient, in my own opinion, is that a healthy Christian perspective should also increase our love and appreciation for our fellow man rather than lead us down the path of judgment. Such a book should rouse us to exercise love and kindness toward each other—as Jesus Himself said, *"Love your neighbor as yourself."* Though we find this statement in the Gospels, this observance wasn't new to Jesus' era; in fact, it harkens back to Leviticus. In other words, loving *people* isn't something we just do in the interests of engendering civility and cordiality in today's modern world; it was part of God's original Law.

In the pages of *God's Wrath Is Good News*, Dave communicates all of these things and more. Through years of study, he has unearthed one of the greatest, one of the most profound, and dare I say one of the most *overlooked* truths of the Gospel. In considering the life and death of Jesus, and all that He came to this earth to accomplish on our behalf, we sometimes miss the most important part of the story—the heart of God, His compassion, His grace, and His insatiable desire for relationship.

You see, there is an unavoidable dichotomy presented in the pages of the New Testament that has been many a Christian's stumbling block in coming to terms with the inexpressible act of love completed on the Cross. On the one hand, God is a loving Father who sent his only Son to die on our behalf so that we could live free of the consequences of sin and death. On the other hand, God is a righteous God who, by His very nature, cannot ignore those same consequences. The beauty of God's great act of love is that, though we deserve death, as Christians we will never taste it. By sending His Son in our place, He ensured that.

When we think of the Gospel, we think of the Cross. What Dave reminds us is that the Gospel did not end there. In fact, the final book of the Bible, Revelation, is also a presentation of the Gospel message—and from the pages of Matthew to the pages of Revelation, that Gospel did not change.

But herein lies the dichotomy, the stumbling block. If the Gospel message does not change or alter from start to finish, why then does Revelation offer us glimpses of death and destruction rather than hope and love? If God has cast our sins upon His Son, freeing us from the consequences of those sins, why then does He send the four horsemen of the apocalypse to ravage the earth in the final days? The answer is that we have fundamentally misunderstood the language of the New Testament as it pertains to the wrath of God. In fact, the wrath of God is not what we think it is at all! The message of God's wrath, the one we absorbed going back to our years of Sunday School, was just plain wrong.

In this book, Dave will take you on a journey of discovery, allowing you to connect for the first time with the truth of God's wrath—and understand once and for all just what the target of God's wrath truly is. Who are the "children of wrath" that Paul talks about in Ephesians? Here's a preview of what's to come—you, as a believer, are not such a child.

The God depicted in this book is not the hot-and-cold, loving-but-judgmental God so often portrayed by the modern Christian church. This is a God you can fall in love with as you come to understand the depth of His passion for you. In fact, the passion of God is so infectious that—as I alluded to a few paragraphs ago—it will cause you to re-evaluate your love for your fellow man. When I finished reading this book, I found myself looking at the world in a whole new light, looking at people and wondering to myself, *What does God think about them?* Of course, there is nothing to wonder about; God's opinion of us, each and every one of us, is as unchangeable as bedrock.

—EVAN BRAUN
Editor, October 2010

CONTENTS

PART THREE

INTRODUCTION

Atheologian of the past, Gustav Sthalin, suggests that God's wrath causes him to network with Satan. In an article published in *The Theological Dictionary of the New Testament,* Sthalin states, "The power and authority of Satan and his hosts are grounded in God's wrath." He then goes on to state, "The devil is never more than God's bailiff. Unwittingly and unwillingly he has become an instrument of the wrath of God whose functions he has only apparently taken under his own wing."[1]

If God allows the devil to be his bailiff, thereby networking with Satan, the kingpin of evil, how can God claim to be holy? If God networks with Satan, he is then involved with evil. How can he then find fault with the

---

[1] *Theological Dictionary of the New Testament*, Volume 5, pp. 439–440.

human race, or pass judgment on us for our involvement and participation in evil?

Sthalin's statement contradicts Jesus' own teachings. Jesus said in Matthew 12:25, *"Every kingdom divided against itself is brought to desolation, and every city or house divided against itself will not stand."* Jesus spoke these words when he was accused of healing a person through the power of Satan. By his statement, Jesus indicates that Satan's kingdom is not about doing good deeds. Jesus declares that Satan comes as a thief *"to steal, and to kill, and to destroy"* (John 10:10). In contrast, Jesus declares that he came to bring abundant life. Therefore Satan's kingdom is represented by everything that is evil. On the other hand, God's kingdom is known by that which is life-giving and good.

The words of Jesus in Matthew very clearly indicate that God's kingdom and Satan's kingdom are mutually exclusive, and totally separate. Therefore, to say that God networks with Satan is to suggest that God and Satan are the expressions of a split personality. The words of Jesus tell us that if God uses Satan as a bailiff, God's kingdom would self-destruct. We must therefore conclude that God does not express his wrath in the same way that Satan does. Nor does God in any way use Satan as a bailiff.

Jesus' words clearly establish that God and Satan represent two very different kingdoms. Yet Scripture uses the same word to speak of God's, Satan's, and humanity's wrath.[2] So how do we define and understand the word

---

[2] In the Greek text, the words used are *orge* and *thumos*. See Strong's Concordance #3709 and #2372.

"wrath" when it is used in reference to God? The way some theologians have understood that word has produced some very strong hellfire and brimstone preaching. In the same vein, the references to God's wrath in the book of Revelation (the last book of the Bible) have been used as fuel for some very graphic fictional portrayals of unprecedented devastation and destruction. These fictional portrayals directly or indirectly suggest that it is God who allows, initiates, or oversees this destruction. Do these fictional portrayals present us with a sound theology and a true portrayal of God's wrath? Some theologians suggest they do. If so, how does that affect the gospel presentation of God as a loving, gracious, and merciful father? Do these fictional portrayals give us an accurate picture of God? Is this the kind of father whose desire it is to redeem our lives from destruction? Is God like a dysfunctional father? Does God have a split personality like Dr. Jekyll and Mr. Hyde? Is God selective in who he redeems? Surely not! So why haven't theologians given us a clearer understanding of God's wrath?

Consider this scenario: you are a witness to child abuse. Your immediate response is anger. What triggered that response? Is your response a mere emotional outburst, or does your response to the abuse go deeper than your emotions? If your response goes beyond emotionalism, it could then be called "wrath."

Wrath is not merely an angry emotional outburst against an experienced or observed injustice. Wrath is grounded in and arises out of a person's character—specifically their love, desire, and will. What if it was your own child who was being abused? The intensity of your anger would then be determined by how much you love your child. Your anger is not driven by a personal hatred of one specific person. It is the abuse more than the abuser that is the focus of your wrath. You want such abuse to stop, and love for your child is the driving force which motivates your wrath. This illustration gives us a glimpse into God's wrath.

Wrath has a negative and positive polarity. The negative pole, which is anger, is directed towards something and/or someone. This negative pole is often focused on the wrong done more so than on the wrong doer. However, it is often the positive pole—love, desire, or will—that determines the intensity and characteristics of wrath.

If you have access to a dictionary published in the early 1900s, you will likely find the word "passion" used as a synonym for "wrath." Modern dictionaries do not use the word "passion" as a synonym for wrath. Instead, they focus on the negative pole of wrath, which is "anger." However, when the word wrath is used in relationship to God, we must keep in mind that it always has a positive motivational force. This positive motivational force can correctly be called passionate desire.

An example of this can be found in John 2:17. In this text, we are told about Jesus making a whip and driving moneychangers from the temple. John does not indicate that Jesus was settling a personal score or that he sought revenge against the moneychangers. However, John clearly indicates that Jesus had a zeal, a passionate desire, for what the temple was to be used for. The text indicates that the temple was built for a specific purpose—namely, prayer. The moneychangers were using the temple for something other than its intended purpose. So Jesus drove the moneychangers from the temple. The actions of Jesus were not so much an expression of anger against the moneychangers as they were an expression of zeal for keeping the temple holy, and used for its intended purpose.

The Bible presents our human wrath as being unrighteous. Our love, desire, and will, representing the positive polarity of our wrath, is often selfishly motivated. For this reason, Paul classifies human *"outbursts of wrath"* as a work of the flesh (Galatians 5:20). "The flesh," according to Paul, constitutes being given to degrading, selfish, baser desires. In contrast, God is stated to be Spirit, not flesh! (1 John 4:24) This fact suggests that God is of a different essence than we are. Therefore, we can be assured that his wrath is not selfishly motivated. Since God is Spirit, his wrath is not motivated by the flesh, and therefore God will always keep the positive and negative polarities of his wrath in proper focus and prospective. For this reason, scripture indicates that God's wrath is *"true and righteous"* (Revelation 16:7). We must therefore conclude that human wrath and God's wrath cannot be the same. God's love, desire, and will, which motivate his wrath, must be held to be holy, just, and righteous.

When we consider God's wrath and Satan's wrath, we can correctly assume that Satan's character is not the same as God's. It is therefore self-evident that God's and Satan's wrath cannot be the same. However, as already noted, scripture uses the same terms to speak of God's, Satan's, and humanity's wrath. Therefore, we must accept that it is the individual person and their character which defines their personal wrath. If we do not keep this distinction in mind, we can mistakenly read the Bible thinking that God's wrath is like ours, or even like Satan's. It may well be that this kind of thinking led to a faulty theology—like Stahlin's, for example.

Stahlin may have based his statements about God's anger on what is written in the Old Testament rather than what is revealed in the New Testament. However, biblical scholars are agreed that the Old Testament is not the final word on God's character. The Old Testament does not give us a full picture of God's love, desire, and will for all people. Therefore, it should not be considered to be the final word on God's wrath.

It is true that the Old Testament clearly indicates that God is opposed to human sin and depravity! However, has our reading of the Old Testament caused us to come to the conclusion that God's negative expressions, manifestations, and enforcement of the Old Testament law are the things that define his wrath? If God's wrath is defined by its negative polarity, what do we do with the revelation of God's love, desire, and will as revealed in the story of Jesus in the New Testament? It is in the story of Jesus, his teachings, and his death on the cross that we are given a more complete picture of God's love, will, and desire for humanity. This fact suggests that the Old Testament does not provide a complete picture of God's wrath, because it does not reveal anything about the positive motivation behind God's wrath.

Appealing to the Old Testament for a definition of God's wrath is like appealing to the law for a definition of love. The Old Testament deals with God's law. The law only defines and clarifies the negative polarity of God's wrath. The law is incapable of defining the positive pole. Nevertheless, the law had a purpose. It served as a tutor and guardian to bring us to the time of Jesus Christ and a fuller revelation of God's character (see Galatians 3:21–29).

Since the New Testament gives us a more complete understanding of God's love, desire, and will, we are compelled to examine what the New Testament says about God's wrath. Theologians are agreed that it is in the New Testament that we are given a fuller understanding of the positive motivation behind God's wrath. Therefore we must take into account God's character, as revealed in the entire Bible, in order to understand God's wrath.

PART
ONE

1

God's Wrath
Is Revealed

There is only one verse in the entire Bible that specifically speaks of the revelation of God's wrath.
That one and only text is Romans 1:18, where
Paul states, *"For the wrath of God is revealed from heaven
against all ungodliness and unrighteousness of men, who suppress the truth in unrighteousness."*

The word "revealed" speaks of the act of taking off a
cover. Paul's use of this word suggests that what is revealed is seen in its entirety for the first time. His use of
this word suggests that God's wrath is seen in its com-
pleteness. His one and only use of the term in the New
Testament also suggests that the Old Testament and the
law did not provide a *complete* revelation of that wrath.

Since the Romans text is the one and only text within
the Bible that speaks of the revelation of God's wrath, it
becomes the key for a correct understanding of God's

wrath. How we understand and apply the word "revealed" determines how we understand the wrath of God. If there is a flaw in our understanding of what Paul is saying, that flaw creates a fault line in our theology.

Is there a fault line in our theology concerning God's wrath? That question can be answered by asking another question. Does the reading of Romans 1:18 produce a *fear of* God or *faith in* God? Undoubtedly, Paul's intention for stating what he wrote was to bring people to faith. So if this passage produces a *fear of* God rather than *faith in* God, you could be misunderstanding the passage.

In Romans 1:16, Paul states, *"I am not ashamed of the gospel of Christ."* Biblical scholars believe Paul to be the best of the New Testament writers. Paul's purpose for writing was to properly present the gospel (good news) in order that people would come to faith in God. We can then correctly assume that Paul's purpose was to bring people to faith with his statement concerning the revelation of God's wrath. Since Paul's statement is part of the New Testament, which is known as the gospel, it must be the presentation of good news.

However, theologians have not always presented Romans 1:18 as good news. Romans 1:18 is often used to point out that God is angry with sinners. And those who use Romans 1:18 for that purpose would probably argue that a healthy fear of God's anger is beneficial. But John tells us that *"fear involves torment"* (1 John 4:18). Paul clearly states that *"the goodness of God leads you to repentance"* (Romans 2:4). Therefore, being afraid of God is not a sound foundation on which to build faith in God. So if our

theology concerning Romans 1:18 produces a fear of God
rather than faith in God, there might well be a fault line in
our understanding of God's wrath.

As noted above, Paul asserted that he was *"not
ashamed of the gospel of Christ"* (Romans 1:16). Paul follows
this declaration with three reasons, which are like suppor-
tive pillars upon which his confidence in the gospel rests.
Those three reasons are:

1. The gospel *"is the power of God to
   salvation"* (1:16).
2. The gospel reveals the righteousness of
   God (1:17).
3. *"The wrath of God is revealed from heaven
   against all ungodliness and unrighteousness of
   men"* (1:18).

Paul's thesis in this text is to show that he is not
ashamed of the gospel. He makes this declaration, then
gives three reasons for making it. The third reason, like the
first and second, indicates that with the coming of Jesus
Christ God has changed the way in which he deals with
humans. The Old Testament law held everyone responsible for their sins. Therefore, under the Old Testament
economy there was no escape from condemnation and the
sentence of death. The coming of the gospel of Christ has
changed that, and one of the primary reasons for that
change is that God's wrath is revealed against all ungodliness and unrighteousness of men. Unlike the Old Testament, in which God repeatedly dealt with the transgres-

sions of men according to the law, Paul's statement indicates that with the advent of the gospel the issue of ungodliness and unrighteousness is dealt with once and for all.

Theologians accept Romans 1:18 as proclaiming that God's wrath against sin is revealed in Christ's death on the cross. Therefore, Jesus Christ's death became our redemption, and Romans 1:18 is accepted as pointing to this gospel truth.

On the other hand, many also see Paul's statement concerning the revelation of God's wrath as an indication that God is still angry with sinners. They hold that God is holy and cannot tolerate sin, and therefore he will punish sinners. Such a theology divides the gospel into good news and bad news.

The gospel is then marked by a fault line. It presents God's wrath like two geological plates pushing in opposite directions. On the one hand, it presents God as a loving, caring father who wants to save people from destruction, but on the other hand, if they don't accept the message of the gospel God himself will seek to destroy them. Is this the kind of father Jesus presented God to be like? Is the gospel both good and bad news?

Each of Paul's three reasons for not being ashamed of the gospel is followed by a further clarification of that point—that the gospel is the *"power of God to salvation"* is stated to be true *"for everyone who believes, for the Jew first and also for the Greek"* (Romans 1:16). With this statement, Paul establishes that with the advent of the gospel there is no differentiation between Jew and Gentile. In Jesus Christ, God does not favour or give preferential treatment to one race over another, as appears to be the case in the Old Testament. The gospel declares God's purpose and plan *for every human being*. In Jesus Christ, God has chosen all people for salvation from destruction and death.

Paul's second reason for not being ashamed of the gospel is that it reveals the righteousness of God by faith. Under the Old Testament economy, a person was considered righteous according to how well they could live out the requirements of the law. With the advent of Jesus Christ, a new economy came into being. Instead of righteousness being based upon a person's ability to keep the law, righteousness is now based upon *a person's faith in what God has already done for us in Christ Jesus on the cross*, as revealed in the gospel. Under this new economy, righteousness is not measured by a person's adherence to prescribed religious behaviour. Faith in God and what Jesus Christ did on the cross changes a person's character—their heart, soul, and spirit—which in turn changes their behaviour. The law is not capable of changing character, but faith in Jesus Christ does.

Paul's third and primary reason for not being ashamed of the gospel is that God's wrath is revealed against ungodliness and unrighteousness. With the sacrifice of Jesus as *"the Lamb of God who takes away the sin of the world"* (John 1:29), God's anger against the sinner has been appeased. Paul states, *"God was in Christ reconciling the world to Himself"* (2 Corinthians 5:19).

In Jesus Christ's death on the cross, God was dealing with the ungodliness and unrighteousness of all people. Isaiah 53:5 states that *"he [Jesus] was pierced for our transgres-*

sions, he was crushed for our iniquities; the punishment that brought us peace was upon him" (NIV). Then Isaiah 53:6 adds, "We all, like sheep, have gone astray, each of us turned to his own way; and the Lord has laid on him [Jesus] the iniquity of us all" (NIV). Therefore, with the advent of the gospel, it is established that all people are the object of God's love. It is God's will and desire that all sinners come to a place of repentance rather than follow their selfish desires, which lead to evil and self-destruction.

Some theologians have presented Paul's third reason for not being ashamed of the gospel as an indictment against those who do not exercise faith. This implies that Paul is saying God's wrath is revealed in opposition to those without faith. However, in this passage, Paul says nothing about the suppression of faith, or the lack of faith. Instead, Paul addresses the ungodliness and unrighteousness of humanity, which came about because they suppressed the truth about God. This indicates that the revelation of God's wrath is not a response to those without faith. Instead, this revelation of God's wrath deals with ungodliness and unrighteousness, which was the result of humanity suppressing the truth about God. Since Paul has stated that this ungodliness and unrighteousness is the result of suppressing the truth about God, the burning question is, "What truth about God is addressed in the revelation of his wrath that is not revealed in the Old Testament?"

By making his statement concerning the revelation of God's wrath part of the gospel, Paul is implying that until the advent of the gospel there was not a clear understanding of God and his wrath. Paul's statement also implies that this revelation brought a truth to humanity about God that was neither known through the law, nor through our observation of creation. So what is the truth about God which is revealed in the New Testament but is not found in the Old Testament or observed in creation? The question suggests that if our theology presents a gospel that does not give a clear understanding of what God revealed, our presentation of the gospel is a suppression of the truth. Therefore, the proclamation of the gospel must be a clear and distinct presentation of good news.

A Study of the Word "Revealed"

In Romans 1:16–18, Paul highlights the revelation of God's wrath as being one of three pillars upon which his confidence in the gospel rests. Paul parallels the revelation of God's wrath with God's provision of salvation and righteousness. If the revelation of God's wrath is not good news, how then could Paul speak of it as part of the gospel?

In order to come to understand the revelation of God's wrath, we need to understand what Paul was implying by his use of the word "revealed." Paul uses this word in both verses seventeen and eighteen. In the Greek text, these verbs are identical—they are identical in tense, voice, mood, person, and number. Proper biblical exegesis (interpretation) demands that what we hold the word to refer to in verse seventeen has to be equally true for its use in verse eighteen. Therefore, to understand Paul's statement regarding the revelation of God's wrath, we must establish a clear understanding of how "revealed" is used in verse seventeen. How the word is used in verse seventeen must then be applied to how it is to be understood in verse eighteen.

It is obvious that the word "revealed," as used in Romans 1:17, points to what theologians designate as special revelation. In the text, Paul makes a distinction between what theologians call "special" revelation and "general" revelation. Paul refers to general revelation when he states, *"What may be known of God is manifest in them, for God has shown it to them. For since the creation of the world His invisible attributes are clearly seen, being understood by the things that are made"* (Romans 1:19–20). Paul uses the word "manifest" to designate the act by which the created world shows the existence of God as creator. The term "manifest" designates general revelation, and general revelation designates those things which we understand and know about God by our observation of the universe.

Theologians set special revelation apart from general revelation. Special revelation refers to those things that cannot be known by human observation. In special revelation, God himself reveals something to us because we can't know or understand it without that special revelation.

This is precisely the case in respect to righteousness. Throughout his writings, Paul repeatedly points out that righteousness did not come by the law, or by keeping the law (Galatians 2:21, 3:21, and Philippians 3:9). Paul makes it very clear that *"one believes unto righteousness"* (Romans 10:10). Righteousness is a matter of faith (Romans 9:30). It is by means of our faith in Jesus Christ that we *"become the righteousness of God"* (2 Corinthians 5:21). Without question, we must conclude that Paul's use of the word "revealed" in Romans 1:17 points to a divine act initiated and completed by God alone. Without the revelation of Jesus Christ as the Lamb, who took away sin, and our acceptance of that by faith, there is no possibility of humanity being declared righteous. Paul's point is clear: when you believe that God reconciled you unto himself in Christ Jesus, God declares you righteous (2 Corinthians 5:19–21).

This strongly suggests that Paul is using the word "revealed" in verse seventeen to designate special revelation. Apart from the special revelation of Jesus Christ, our attempts at being righteous by keeping the law are futile. So, Paul's use of the word "revealed" in verse seventeen references our faith being placed in the special revelation of Jesus Christ.

Paul's use of this identical word in verse eighteen indicates that when he is speaking of the revelation of God's wrath he is speaking about special revelation. To see Paul's use of the word "revealed" in verse eighteen as general revelation ignores Paul's use of a very specific technical term. Paul's repeated use of the identical word used in verse seventeen indicates that Paul is not speaking about something we observe about God, but something that God himself has shown us. For the word "revealed" to be considered anything other than special revelation in verse eighteen, it must be shown that Paul had no intention of paralleling it with the previous verse. If theologians deny such a parallel, they must then explain why Paul uses this term to designate special revelation in verse seventeen but doesn't do so again in verse eighteen. To say that the word "revealed" of verse seventeen has no bearing on its meaning in verse eighteen defies all rules of sound biblical understanding and interpretation.

Theologians have presented God's judgments of the Old Testament as revealing God's wrath. However, Paul's use of the word "revealed," which points to special revelation, argues otherwise. What God's wrath is against is clearly manifested by the application of the Old Testament law and the acts by which that law was enforced. However, the enforcement of that law only established the negative polarity of God's wrath. The positive motivation behind God's wrath is not revealed by the judgments carried out in the Old Testament, just like God's call to righteousness and holiness is not fully revealed by the keeping of the Old Testament law. It is impossible for the law to express the fullness of God's love, will, and desire for humanity, and it is God's love, will, and desire for humanity that is the motivation behind the revelation of his wrath.

Paul's repeated use of the word "revealed" in verse eighteen indicates that God's wrath could not be known or understood apart from special revelation, just like righteousness could not be attained apart from the special revelation of Jesus Christ. Therefore, just as Jesus Christ is at the heart of the revelation of God's righteousness, so is he at the heart of the revelation of God's wrath. Jesus Christ's death on the cross is the personification of all of God's anger against sin, while at the same time it is a revelation of God's profound love for the sinner.

2

God's Revealed Wrath Is the Foundation of the Gospel

Jesus came to earth because of God's love for the world, and this love is what gives life to the gospel. God's love for humanity is the positive motivation behind the revelation of his wrath. God's love for humanity accents and clarifies the intensity of both the negative and positive side of God's wrath.

Paul begins with the word "because" in Romans 1:19. "Because" indicates that Paul will now expand on the reason that God revealed his wrath. Paul deemed it more important to explain the *why* of that revelation than the *what*. This suggests that Paul assumed his readers would come to a clear and proper understanding of the *what* of God's revelation after he explained the *why*.

Romans 1:19–20 states, *"Because what may be known of God is manifest in them, for God has shown it to them. For since the creation of the world His invisible attributes are clearly seen, being understood by the things that are made, even His eternal power and Godhead."* Paul is saying that as humans we have knowledge of God. This knowledge comes via our observation of God's creative power, displayed in the universe around us. Paul references this as a manifestation of God. Remember, Paul uses the word "manifest" to indicate what theologians refer to as general revelation. Paul indicates that this general revelation, or manifestation of God in creation, provides us with the knowledge of God's power and divinity. So much so that Paul declares we *"are without excuse"* (Romans 1:20). We cannot plead ignorance about the existence, power, and divinity of God.

But in spite of this observed knowledge about God, humans did not acknowledge or worship God as the divine creator. Instead, humanity suppressed, and continues to suppress, the truth about God as creator. According to Paul, this suppression of truth leads humanity into deeper degenerative behaviour.

In Romans 1:21, Paul continues his thesis with another "because." By this, Paul indicates that humanity's refusal to act on the knowledge gained through general revelation led them into ever increasing ungodliness and unrighteousness. Suppressing the truth about God as the creator leads humanity into ever widening self-destructive behaviour.

Paul's discourse is a concise thesis on our depraved spiritual disposition. Our awareness and knowledge of

God as creator is dismissed as invalid. Since one's knowledge of God is sidelined and ignored, one descends into deeper spiritual darkness, which results in a refusal to acknowledge God or be thankful to God. This rejection of God gives rise to a spiritual blindness that leads to an idolatrous imagination (Romans 1:21). In this condition, humans boast about their wisdom, but in reality they have become fools (Romans 1:22). Paul next outlines how this condition causes humanity to spiral downward into ungodliness and unrighteousness.

How does God respond to the downward spiral of humanity? Like the prodigal son's father of Luke 15, God allows us to follow our own idolatrous imaginations. In the Romans 1 passage, Paul likens people to a drunkard who has taken leave of his or her senses and spirals deeper into self-destructive acts. None of us are immune to these self-destructive acts, and many maintain this foolish course of action fully *"knowing the righteous judgment of God, that those who practice such things are deserving of death"* (Romans1:32). By this statement, Paul indicates that humans agree with God's judgment against sinners: they *"are deserving of death."* Those who reject God's provision of salvation cannot fault God because of their condition and future prospects. God is not obligated to change in order to accommodate the sinner. But many of those who consciously acknowledge that sinful behaviour deserves death not only continue their sinful action, *"but also approve of those who practice"* such things (Romans 1:32).

Obviously, general revelation—God's manifestation of himself in creation—is not sufficient to arrest humanity's descent into a living hell. Our awareness of God's power and divinity, and our acknowledgment that God is right in his judgment that we are deserving of death, cannot stop our downward spiral. Through experience, we know that the law is not capable of stopping bad behaviour, nor can the law stop us from breaking the law. Therefore, the law is unable to rescue us from acts of self-destruction. The law only enforces the fact that sinful behaviour deserves punishment.

Paul points to the nation of Israel as an example. He points out that even Israel, a nation favoured by God and given the law to govern their action, could not bring their ungodliness under control (Romans 2:1, 17:25). God gave Israel Ten Commandments which were meant to govern their life and keep them holy. These commandments gave Israel a clear understanding of the actions that would neither benefit nor improve their life and were therefore not approved by God. Did Israel stop sinning? No! They failed miserably, and instead of the law being a means of escape from destruction it became their sentence to destruction. So God exercised restraint, mercy, and grace in order to keep from abandoning Israel to their law-breaking, self-destructive actions.

God was fully aware that if he was going to stop humanity's downward spiral into death and destruction, we would require more than the knowledge and experience of the negative polarity of his wrath, as seen in the Old Testament record of the Israelites and the application of the law. This is why God gave us a special revelation of his wrath. This special revelation displays both the negative and positive aspects of God's wrath in their most vivid intensity. God's anger against ungodliness and unrighteousness, and his love for the sinner, are focused and personified in one person: Jesus Christ!

Jesus: The Object of God's Wrath

Jesus came from heaven to deal with sin as only he could. While hanging on the cross, Jesus cried, *"My God, my God, why have You forsaken Me?"* (Matthew 27:46, Mark 15:34) Jesus experienced the wrath of God against sin like no human will ever experience it. Isaiah 53:6 declares that *"the Lord has laid upon Him the iniquity of us all."* And again, in Isaiah 53:11, Isaiah declares, *"My righteous Servant shall justify many, for He shall bear their iniquities."* In the death of Jesus Christ on the cross, we see an unprecedented revelation of God's wrath against sin. This revelation of the wrath of God against sin stands as a beacon for all eternity. This is why Paul speaks of it in the present tense: not *was*, or *will be*, but *"the wrath of God is revealed."* The passing of time cannot erase the efficacy, relevancy, and magnitude of that singular revelation.

Biblical scholars and preachers have tried to help us understand the agony of Jesus' suffering on the cross. They have painted vivid word pictures of every event from Peter's betrayal of Jesus to the nails being driven through his hands and feet and the jolt of pain he felt as the cross was dropped into place. Some of these scenes were vividly portrayed in Mel Gibson's movie, *The Passion of the Christ*.

However, none of these descriptions or scenes could do justice to the true agony that Jesus experienced on the cross. It was agony and heartbreak so intense that it caused him to give up his life.

Scripture tells us that Jesus *"learned obedience by the things which he suffered"* (Hebrews 5:8). We assume this verse speaks of Jesus learning to be obedient to his father. Not so! Scripture tells us that Jesus always did what he saw his father do. He came to do his father's will (John 6:38). So what did he have to learn obedience to?

As the son of the eternal God, he *"became obedient to the point of death, even the death of the cross"* (Philippians 2:8). Can you fathom it? Jesus the son of God—Divinity, the source of life—became obedient to death.

Can you comprehend the son of God dying and his Father appearing to remain impotent and unable to rescue him from death? But that is what the biblical record indicates; Jesus was equal with God his father (Philippians 2:5). Like the father, he was life! And above all, he and his father had a perfect relationship. "Yet no one ever plunged down into the vacuum of evil as did Jesus."[3] We will never know or understand the excruciating crushing, life-robbing pain behind the words, *"My God, My God, why have You forsaken me?"*

It is not my intention to diminish or downplay the physical trauma that Jesus endured. However, the cry of anguish from Jesus before giving up in spirit goes beyond any physical pain or trauma. Jesus anticipated this agony

---

[3] Manning, p. 71.

when he prayed, *"If it be possible, let this cup pass from Me"* (Matthew 26:39). He wasn't praying to be released from the physical suffering of the crucifixion. His prayer concerned something deeper and more agonizing than any physical pain recorded in history. He was able to deal with Judas' betrayal, Peter's denial, and the mockery of a so-called trial. He endured the pain of being beaten, the crown of thorns placed on his head, and the nails driven through his body. In fact, he prayed, *"Father, forgive them, for they do not know what they do"* (Luke 23:34).

Matthew tells us that shortly after Jesus cried, *"My God, My God, why have You forsaken me?"* he *"yielded up His spirit"* (Matthew 27:50). Mark also records that Jesus cried out and then breathed his last breath. (Mark 15:37). Jesus was able to fight through his physical mistreatment. However, the weight of carrying our unrighteousness and ungodliness brought on a feeling of being abandoned by his father. Bearing our grief and carrying our sorrows blotted out the face and favour of his father. Carrying our transgressions and iniquities blinded him to being able to see God as father. Can a loving, caring father abandon his son? God appears to have abandoned his only son on the cross, and it caused Jesus to give up in his spirit and become obedient to death.

Isaiah indicates that it wasn't God the father who was punishing him. *"We esteemed Him stricken, smitten by God, and afflicted. But He was wounded for our transgressions"* (Isaiah 53:4–5). God the father didn't put him on the cross. Our sin nailed him there! And the atrocities inflicted on Jesus by those who mocked and killed him forever speak to us of our sinfulness. He need not have suffered, but for this cause he was born. Sin leads to death, which is to be separated from God, the source of life. So Jesus tasted *"death for everyone"* (Hebrews 2:9). He drained the cup of separation from his father so that *"through death He might destroy him who had the power of death, that is, the devil"* (Hebrews 2:14). So it is in Jesus' cry of abandonment that God's wrath against sin is forever revealed.

We as humans may be able to identify with the physical pain and suffering that Jesus endured. However, those who have suffered the pain of a broken relationship—such as divorce, or a parent leaving and abandoning them—understand a little more of what Jesus was going through when he cried, *"My God, My God, why have You forsaken me?"* The pain and agony of feeling abandoned by the ones you love and with whom you have a perfect relationship is unspeakable. This kind of pain is indescribable! Yet from this very point on the cross comes a cry that should touch us at our very core. In it, we are given a glimpse into the revelation of God's wrath against sin. Jesus' cry of being forsaken by his father reveals the negative polarity of God's wrath in its deepest extreme. The depth of God's anger against the sins of humanity is seen in the moment where the father does not deliver his own son from death. There is no effort to rescue him from experiencing such a fate. Jesus' feeling of abandonment caused him to draw his last breath. Amazingly, at the point of Jesus' deepest anguish, we see the astonishing intensity of the positive motivation behind God's wrath, his passionate love for us. God, the source of all life, withholds life from his own son and allows him to die in order to give us life. The cross is a constant witness to the revelation of God's wrath against ungodliness and unrighteousness in every human being.

Paul does not specifically say that the gospel reveals God's wrath against sin. Rightly so! There are no words that could express the agony of abandonment felt by Jesus on the cross. Nor could we comprehend the torment that God the father endured in putting his only son through such agony. This act is beyond mere words and human comprehension. Yet that is the very heart of the gospel! No amount of human suffering could atone for human ungodliness and unrighteousness. So Jesus did it for us all! Jesus became the object of God's anger against the sinner. Jesus endured separation from his father in order that we need not be separated from his father ever again. Without this revelation of God's wrath at the cross, there is no gospel! No wonder Paul unashamedly speaks of the revelation of God's wrath in relationship to the gospel.

Jesus' cry from the cross displays the truth and holiness of the gospel. The law's demand for sin's punishment necessitated the death of the sinner. Jesus became sin for us and suffered the full penalty of the law. Thereby, Jesus fulfilled the requirements of the law, and God's demand for atonement was fulfilled. Consequently, John could boldly declare, *"He Himself is the propitiation for our sins, and not for ours only but also for the whole world"* (1 John 2:2). Jesus Christ's death on the cross reveals the wrath of God against our sin for all eternity. There is no other person or event that could satisfy God, nor is there any other person or event that could meet the requirements to fulfill God's demand for justice and righteousness. To suggest that God could be satisfied by any other event or person other than Jesus Christ is to make a mockery of the cross and the gospel.

So this is the good news of the gospel. In Christ Jesus, God's wrath against you and me as sinners has been satisfied. This brings the pregnancy of the positive polarity of God's wrath to full term. It is in this indescribable revelation of the negative polarity that we are brought face to face with the positive motivation behind God's wrath—his love for us! This revelation is all-sufficient for everyone and for all time. It is a revelation that cannot be replaced or duplicated. This special revelation of God's wrath against sin provides the foundation upon which the good news of the gospel and the establishment of God's kingdom rest. So let's note it as recorded for time and eternity. The revelation of God's wrath and the establishment of God's kingdom are anchored and realized in God's redemptive work—the death of his son on the cross.

3

God's Wrath Is Revealed from Heaven

Paul states that God's wrath is revealed *"from heaven."* Paul has already ascribed this wrath to God by the genitive *"of God,"* so why add *"from heaven"*?

"From heaven" is a phrase used throughout the New Testament. Jesus is authenticated as God's beloved son by a voice from heaven (Mark 1:11). Paul, at the time of his transformation in character, sees a light from heaven (Acts 9:3, 22:6). Jesus speaks of Himself as the bread that came down from heaven (John 6:32–35). The Holy Spirit is sent down from heaven (1 Peter 1:12). Paul speaks of the house we long to be clothed with as coming from heaven (2 Corinthians 5:2). So that which is revealed or comes *"from heaven"* has nothing in common with anything in this world. *"From heaven"* is a phrase that identifies what is being referred to as not of this world, not influenced or contaminated by this world, and which comes from a totally

different source than everything we have known or experienced in this world.

In Acts 11, that which originates in heaven is identified
as having nothing in common with anything of this world,
even though it appears and looks like something from this
world. Peter sees a vision in which various creatures are
lowered from heaven (Acts 11:6). He is commanded to
"kill and eat" (Acts 11:7). Peter objects on the grounds that
he has never eaten anything common or unclean. He then
hears a voice from heaven stating, *"What God has cleansed
you must not call common"* (Acts 11:9).

Peter's vision suggests that even though we may view
something on earth as common, unclean, or defiled, when
it comes from heaven it has been cleansed. God's wrath
originated from heaven; therefore, it is not common. It is
not contaminated and defiled like the wrath we experience
in this world. And above all, it is not like human or Satan's
wrath, even though the same terms are used for each.

Isaiah 55:8–9 states, *"'For My thoughts are not your
thoughts, nor are your ways My ways,' says the Lord. 'For as the
heavens are higher than the earth, so are My ways higher than
your ways, and My thoughts than your thoughts.'"* Obviously,
heaven is a place totally separated from everything on this
earth. Heaven is where God's will is done (Matthew 6:10).
What originates and is revealed from heaven of necessity
has God's will in proper perspective. That which is revealed from heaven has at its heart God's will, purpose,
and plan, and above all is motivated by his love.

So we must conclude that the source determines quality. Therefore, *"from heaven"* designates God's wrath as

being impeccable in quality. *"From heaven"* places God's wrath in a category of its own. We should not compare or liken it to any other type of wrath. *"From heaven"* sets God's wrath apart from all other types of wrath. God's wrath is from a totally different realm and source than ours or Satan's. It is also of a totally different nature, essence, and purpose than that of ours or Satan's. Thus, Acts 11:9 could be rephrased as, *"The wrath that God reveals from heaven should be understood as having nothing in common with the wrath that we have experienced in this world."*

God's wrath is as far removed from ours as heaven is from earth. Since there is not a full revelation of God's righteousness in the Old Testament, neither is there a full revelation of God's wrath in the Old Testament. It bears repeating: The genitive *"of God"* coupled with *"from heaven"* sets God's wrath apart from all other types of wrath. God's wrath is motivated by his love, will, and desire. God's wrath cannot be opposed to his character. God's wrath is grounded and anchored in his love, mercy, grace, and holiness. It is therefore paramount that when we read the phrase *"wrath of God"* in the New Testament, we see it in light of God's character as revealed in Jesus Christ. So, mark it! God's wrath is revealed from heaven and is therefore unlike any wrath we have experienced in this world. It is so unlike the wrath of this world that God revealed it to us by way of special revelation, in order that we fully understand it.

God's Wrath Has a Negative Polarity

God's wrath, which is revealed from heaven, has a negative polarity. Paul tells us what that negative polarity is. It is revealed *"against all ungodliness and unrighteousness of men"* (Romans 1:18). What makes God angry? Many theologians have taken the genitive phrase *"of men"* as indicating that humans are the object of God's anger. The characteristics of ungodliness and unrighteousness have been understood as modifiers of the term *"men."* But look at the text carefully! Paul does not say, "God's wrath is revealed against all people of ungodliness and unrighteousness." Paul clearly indicates that the negative object or focus of God's wrath is ungodliness and unrighteousness. *"Of men"* is the genitive modifier for the phrase *"ungodliness and unrighteousness."*

God is not angry with you as a person and is therefore not seeking to destroy you as a person. It is the ungodliness and unrighteousness that God is angry about, and it is this ungodliness and unrighteousness that keeps you from being who God created you to be. God's intention is to separate you from your negative, degrading, and destructive behaviour. God wants to liberate you so you can live free of condemnation and self-destructive behaviour.

In Romans 1:18, the genitive modifier *"of men"* explains whose ungodliness and unrighteousness God is dealing with in the revelation of his wrath. According to the Bible, God's creation was not originally defiled by humanity. The biblical record indicates that ungodliness and unrighteousness did not begin with people; it began with

Satan. Therefore, *"of men"* appears to be a restrictive genitive. As a restrictive genitive, it indicates there is a limitation to whose ungodliness and unrighteousness God is dealing with in the revelation of his wrath. The revelation that Paul is addressing here does not include Satan's ungodliness; it is limited to humanity's. The negative polarity of God's wrath is focused against Satan, who causes humans to sin.

The gospel message is clear: Jesus dealt with humanity's sins. It is Satan and his action that will be judged and dealt with in the future. People who insist on being *"children of wrath"* (look ahead to Chapter 5) have cast their lot with Satan and will suffer the same consequences he will.

What About God's Abiding Wrath?

But what about scriptures that speak about God's wrath abiding on the person? Theologians of the past have understood this to imply that God continues to be angry with sinners and is therefore actively seeking to punish them. However, consider this: Is it God's intention to destroy sin by destroying the sinner? If that is the purpose of God's abiding wrath, then the God of the Bible is no different from any other god of literature. Such thinking negates Paul's statement that *"Christ Jesus came into the world to save sinners"* (1 Timothy 1:15).

John 3:17 declares that *"God did not send His Son into the world to condemn the world, but that the world through Him might be saved."* The heart of the gospel message clearly indicates that God wants to change the world through the redemption of sinners, not by their destruction. This is what makes the gospel unique amongst the religions of the world.

Yet some theologians continue to insist that it is God's intention to destroy evil by destroying the sinner. Preachers who believe this have relied on "hellfire and brimstone preaching." These preachers believe that sinners are brought to repentance by instilling in them a fear of God's wrath. However, Paul's theology suggests the opposite. Paul declares that *"the goodness of God leads [us] to repentance"* (Romans 2:4).

It should be noted that when scripture speaks of God's abiding wrath it always makes mention of a person's unrighteous action. For example, in John 3:36, John the Baptist speaks of those who do not believe in the Son as not having life. Rather, he states that the wrath of God abides on them because of their unbelief. Paul maintains this point in both Ephesians 5:6 and Colossians 3:6. In both of these passages, Paul indicates that the wrath of God comes on the children of disobedience *"because of these things."* *"These things"* is a reference to the deeds of sinful humanity, which are referred to as deeds of the flesh (Galatians 5:19–20). Thus it is not the individual that is singled out as the specific object of God's wrath. The negative force of God's wrath is said to be directed against unbelief and action of the children of disobedience. Since it is the *unbelief* and *sinful action* of the individual, and not the individual himself, that is the focus of God's anger, God's foremost desire must be to separate the disobedient person from his or her action.

Neither John the Baptist nor Paul specifies how the wrath of God is manifested or carried out in the above mentioned scriptures. In Romans 1:24–28, Paul specifically states that God gives people up to their depraved nature and thereby indicates that God does not force his will on anyone. This suggests that God's wrath against sin causes him to become indifferent to the disobedient person. God seemingly withdraws and allows that person their choice of evil behaviour, which leads them into ever deeper depravity. Without repentance, this ever deeper depravity becomes that person's road to hell. Jesus distinctly states that *"everlasting fire [was] prepared for the devil and his angels"* (Matthew 25:41). It goes beyond anything that Paul has written to assume that his reference to the revelation of God's wrath suggests an active retaliation carried out by God.

There is one exception to this rule, which is found in Romans 3:5. It is an exception that may establish the rule. Paul asks the question, *"Is God unjust who inflicts wrath?"* The verb that Paul uses here—inflicts—suggests a personal attack, an attack against the individual. However, Paul is quick to clarify that he speaks as a man. Paul is saying that his reference to God inflicting his wrath on the individual comes from his own human perspective. The sinner views God's anger against sin as anger against himself or herself as a person. However, given David Daube's observations concerning this verse, we should probably question such a conclusion.

Daube points out that Paul's statement—*"I speak as a man*—is an apology for saying something bordering on blasphemy.[4] Paul apologizes for saying something about God that is not true. God is not like a human who would take vengeance on the individual. To suggest that God is like a human, and that he responds like a human, borders on blasphemy. So Paul's apology in Romans 3:5 suggests that God is not vengeful or retaliatory.

It is true that we as humans see God's wrath as being levelled against us because we know we have done wrong. However, be assured, God's desire is not to destroy you and he did not create you for the purpose of destruction. God's desire is to redeem you from death and destruction. For this reason, Paul deliberately states that the negative focus of God's wrath is *"unrighteousness and ungodliness"* (Romans 1:18), In Jesus Christ, God's wrath was revealed against ungodliness and unrighteousness with the specific intention of redeeming the person. Paul's point in Romans 1:18 is that God's wrath is redemptive.

And God is unchanging in his nature and purpose.

---

[4] David Daube, p. 396.

PART TWO

4

The Gospel Isn't Good News and Bad News

Religious theology has presented the gospel as both good and bad news. Dr. Martyn Lloyd-Jones is an example of such a theologian.[5] In dealing with the Romans 1 passage, Lloyd-Jones presents the cross as being one of seven ways in which God's wrath is revealed. According to him, the six things, other than the cross, are as follows: 1) our conscience, 2) the consequences of sin, 3) the state of creation, 4) death, 5) history, 6) and the teaching of scripture.[6]

A position such as this allows for the atrocities of wars, the events of 9/11, the invasion of Iraq, World Wars I and

---

[5] It is not my intention to single out Lloyd-Jones. However, I quote him as being representative of theologians who argue for a variety of ways in which God's wrath is revealed. These theologians accept that Paul is referencing Jesus Christ's death on the cross but do not see it as the singular event that reveals God's wrath.

[6] Lloyd-Jones, pp. 342-348.

II, and every other act of man's inhumanity against man to be classified as revelations of God's wrath. However, the first five things that Lloyd-Jones lists are often the result of our own selfish passions. Only one of the six, the teaching of scripture, is in the class of special revelation. Conscience, the consequences of sin, the state of creation, death, and history cannot be classed as special revelation, and for sure they don't originate in heaven. Since the two previous chapters establish that Romans 1:18 is speaking of special revelation, which originates in heaven, we must rule out these five things as revealing God's wrath.

To even suggest that these five stand alongside the cross as a revelation of God's wrath places the revelation of God's wrath in the company of every atrocity committed by humanity. Is that the kind of wrath we expect to be revealed from heaven by one referred to as a heavenly father? To suggest that God's wrath is revealed in the cross of Christ as well as man's inhumanity against man is an affront to God's holiness. Because God is holy (a point that is developed in the next chapter), we must conclude that his wrath has nothing in common with the atrocities we experience in this world. The God of heaven is not fickle like the gods of mythical literature.

Lloyd-Jones asserts that the scriptures reveal God's wrath. I am assuming he means that throughout the Old Testament there have been statements made and examples given of God's actions against sin. However, as already noted, the Old Testament economy—the law—could only portray the negative polarity of God's wrath. It could not reveal the positive motivation behind God's wrath. It is only in the gospel that we are given a divine revelation of this positive side of God's wrath. God's love for you and me was the motivation and reason for revealing that wrath at the cross.

Paul's use of the definite article "the" in Romans 1:18 suggests that Paul is focusing on the singular event that revealed God's wrath. If "the wrath" was to be understood as referencing an Old Testament judgment of sin, or any other event in history (as suggested by Lloyd-Jones), Paul should then have either given an example of it or stated something to that effect. Paul is silent in that regard. Paul says nothing about past or impending punishment by God. In fact, the context of Romans 1:18 suggests the exact opposite course of action on God's part.

In Romans 1, Paul's discourse brings humanity's degenerative behaviour to three successive climaxes. Three times Paul states, *"God gave them up"* (Romans 1:24, 1:26, and 1:28). If there was ever an opportunity for Paul to draw attention to God's wrath being the punishment of the sinner, here is that opportunity. Paul, however, draws no such parallel! God's only recorded action is that he gives humans up to let them follow their own passions. God's act of allowing humanity their free will and desires is presented as a loving father's response to a headstrong child.

Since Paul does not give a concrete example of God's wrath from either the Old Testament or human history, Lloyd-Jones' conclusions about the other six things that reveal God's wrath must be called into question.

Paul's words are not an indictment against us but a factual accounting of our inability to overcome our attraction to sin. We need more than laws and the fear of punishment to keep us from doing wrong. So God gives us a revelation of the positive and negative extremes of his wrath which stands as a beacon for all ages. God's love for you caused him to undertake the most uncommon, incomparable, and unfathomable act of history. He allowed his son to die so you could choose life!

Lloyd-Jones' position is also called into question by the words *"against all ungodliness and unrighteousness of men."* "All" strongly suggests that Paul is presenting this revelation as dealing with all of humanity's past, present, and future ungodliness. Paul's writings clearly indicate that there is only one person and one event which can be seen as accomplishing this for all time and all humanity. That one person is Jesus, and that one event is the cross. To consider any other event, or any other person, as being comparable to this makes Jesus Christ's death on the cross a common, ordinary act of history. The cross then becomes one of many different ways in which God reveals his wrath in order to deal with ungodliness and unrighteousness. But Paul's use of the definite article indicates that he is referencing a singular event that reveals God's wrath, and in that singular event all ungodliness and unrighteousness has been dealt with.

God no longer has a problem with sin! We as humans have a problem with it because we refuse to accept God's provision for it. And thereby we disregard God's awesome love, expressed for us in the passion of the Christ. However, Paul not only accepts but understands the scope of God's provision for our sin, and therefore asserts that he is not ashamed of the gospel. In the death of Jesus Christ, the wrath of God against sin is revealed for all of human history. This sets Romans 1:18 apart as the benchmark for our understanding of the revelation of God's wrath. Paul doesn't specifically spell out what reveals that wrath. He tells us that it is revealed by special revelation. He informs us that the negative polarity of God's wrath is the ungodliness and unrighteousness of humanity. He lets us know that neither Jews nor Gentiles could bring their ungodliness under control. With that, Paul assumes we would come to a proper conclusion concerning the revelation of God's wrath.

Thus, Lloyd-Jones is profoundly correct in saying, "The cross, the death of our Lord and Saviour Jesus Christ" reveals God's wrath, then adds, "There is nothing—there is nothing in history anywhere—which in any way approximates to this as a revelation of the wrath of God."[7] It is precisely because there is nothing in history—past, present, or future—that can be compared to the cross of Christ that the cross of Jesus Christ stands as the one and only reference point for that revelation. The death of Jesus on the cross is the one and only event that meets the criteria of being a special revelation from heaven. Mark it, note it, and never forget it! The revelation of God's wrath is a redemptive act for all people and all history. Without the special revelation of Jesus Christ and God's wrath

---

[7] Ibid., p. 348.

against sin in his son's death on the cross, there is no gospel!

Paul clearly presents the gospel as including the truth that God's wrath was revealed in Christ's death on the cross. Without the death of Jesus, the atonement for sin would have been incomplete. His death satisfied and exceeded the requirements of God's law. God's wrath against sin could not and cannot be appeased by any other means. This is the truth which sets the good news of the New Testament apart from the Old Testament in its portrayal of God's wrath.

The Old Testament dealt with the requirements for appeasing God's wrath, and the law set forth those requirements. It is these requirements which established the fact that human beings could not attain righteousness. Jesus Christ met the requirements of the law; therefore, his sacrifice atoned for every person's ungodliness and unrighteousness. Due to this, Paul boldly declares that he is not ashamed of the gospel. In God's kingdom, the problem of sin has been dealt with, the sacrifice for sin has been offered, and Jesus declared, *"It* is finished" (John 19:30).

5

The Revelation
of God's Wrath
Is a Holy Act

S ince the revelation of God's wrath in the death of
Jesus is redemptive, the continued manifestation
and fruition of that wrath must also be redemptive.
If it is not, God then violates his own scripturally mandated criteria for holiness!

Religion would have us believe that the sinner is the
object of God's anger. This position implies that God either ignores or violates his own biblical standard of holiness. To better understand this point, let us examine the
truth about God's holiness. Then we will examine the
scriptures that have been used to support the religious position that the sinner is the object of God's anger.

God Is Holy

Holiness, like wrath, is marked by adherence to negative and positive criteria. According to the biblical record, the negative criteria require that the thing or person which is declared holy be separated from that which is profane or common. The positive criteria require that which is holy to be dedicated to a singular purpose which is godly, just, and righteous. It is this positive standard, more so than the negative standard, which distinguishes and sets apart that which is declared holy, and that should be especially true in regard to God.

The Old Testament record illustrates the negative and positive standards of holiness. The Old Testament book of Leviticus sets forth the standard of holiness for the vessels used in the temple. The negative requirement is seen in the fact that the temple vessels were never to be used for any common purpose. Any vessel or utensil used for a common purpose was not holy, and therefore was not fit to be used in the temple. The positive standard is seen in that these vessels were made for and dedicated to be used exclusively in the temple for their specific and dedicated purpose. Any other use would violate them and render them unholy. Separation from a common use alone did not constitute holiness. It was the making and dedication of the utensil to an exclusive use in the temple that defined and constituted its holiness.

Given this clear scriptural guideline as to what constitutes holiness, we are obligated to understand this principle as applying to anything or anyone that is declared holy.

Therefore, in applying it to God or human beings, the negative side of holiness is seen in one's aversion to and separation from sin and evil. The positive side is seen in a person's dedication to that which is redemptive, godly, just, and good.

Within the theological community, this understanding of holiness is widely accepted. However, the religious community has placed such an emphasis on the negative standard that it has become short-sighted to, or has even ignored, the all-important positive standard. This is especially true when religion deals with God's actions or with human actions and character.

The church community labours to define holiness on the basis of conduct that is acceptable and not acceptable. But is that what God is asking for when he calls for us to *"be holy, for I am holy"* (1 Peter 1:16)? Religion has caused us to place the emphasis on being separated from wrong deeds and actions. But without being dedicated to right and redemptive action, we are still not holy.

It would be more beneficial to think of the 1 Peter 1:16 statement—*"Be holy, for I am holy"*—as saying, "Be redemptive, for I am redemptive." It is in being redemptive and living out the fruit of the spirit, as recorded in Galatians 5:22, that we are Christ-like and holy. Paul's struggle was with not doing the good he wanted to do (see Romans 7:7–25). It is when we have occasion to be good and redemptive but aren't that we violate our call to be holy.

Religion assumes that any action of God is holy. But it is on this very point that its standard for holiness becomes faulty. Whether utensil or person, that which is designated or called to be holy must meet both the negative and positive standard. If it does not meet those standards, it is not holy!

Religion presents God as being the ultimate example of separation from sin and evil, and rightly so. However, this only demonstrates God's holiness on the basis of the negative standard. Can God be declared holy on meeting just the singular requirement of being separated from sin?

Without holding God to the positive standard, the doctrine of God's holiness is vulnerable to question and debate. This is especially true when theologians argue that God's holiness demands that he punish the sinner. Such reasoning leaves God's claim to holiness open to doubt, because it does not establish the truth of God's holiness on the most important positive standard. To declare God holy solely on the basis of his aversion to sin, while ignoring the positive standard for holiness, suggests that God violates his own scripturally-established standards. Religion does not require God to be committed and dedicated to a holy, just, and righteous action, and this has created a fault line in our theology in regard to God's wrath.

So if God is holy on the basis of his aversion to sin alone, theologians are not being consistent with their own theology. As noted above, it is accepted that God is separated from sin. I will not debate that point! Therefore God fulfills the negative requirement for being holy, but it is the positive standard for holiness that is the most glorious and majestic indicator of God's holiness.

Let us note that the positive requirement calls for the one who is designated as holy to be dedicated to a just and righteous act. It is in the realm of this positive standard that God's holiness outshines any and all others.

Theologians are agreed that scripture establishes the fact that there was no person or action that could atone for human transgressions. So God, in his love for the sinner and his wrath against sin, set himself apart to provide atonement for all sinners. God, in the person of Jesus Christ, redeemed humanity from unavoidable destruction. So the revelation of God's wrath in Jesus Christ's death on the cross is an unprecedented act of holiness. The cross of Jesus Christ sets God and his action apart as the summit of holiness.

It is this positive aspect of God's holiness which has been overlooked or misrepresented by religion. For God to cease being redemptive, or to violate his redemptive provision in any of his actions, God would cease to be holy. For God to inflict punishment upon the sinner, after dedicating himself to providing redemption for that sinner, he must become like any common, ordinary human; the atoning work accomplished by Jesus Christ would therefore be violated and no longer holy. If God's wrath is revealed in the state of creation, death, or history—as suggested by Lloyd-Jones—God has then violated his own biblical standard for holiness. Such action portrays God's wrath as common as human wrath, and God's redemptive act in Jesus Christ is no longer uniquely sacred. If God's wrath against ungodliness is revealed in multiple ways, as suggested by Lloyd-Jones, then we might well ask, "What was the purpose of the cross of Christ?"

Someone may ask, "Are you suggesting that God will not send anyone to hell?"

Let's consider that question!

It is because God willed that none perish that he provided a means of escape. Like Adam and Eve in the garden, each human being is given a choice. You can choose life in Jesus Christ or you can choose to reject what Jesus Christ has provided. By not choosing Jesus Christ's provision for your sins, you choose the opposite by default. God allows for the free will of any and every human to override what he has willed and provided. God limits his sovereignty in regard for each person's will and choices. God will not force you to surrender to him or his will. However, in not surrendering to him, you have chosen to be a "child of wrath," with death and hell therefore being unavoidable. (For an explanation of the phrase "child of wrath," see the topic that follows.)

Scripture is very clear that without repentance, which is a turning away from one's own selfish pursuits, a sinner has cast his lot with the devil, and therefore like the devil he will experience the consequences of being given over to evil.

Scripture clearly indicates that when sin is finished, it brings forth death (James 1:15, Galatians 6:8, Romans 6:23). Your choice will not be overruled by God. God in his holiness provided all people with a means of redemption. The individual who decides not to believe in Christ is condemned already (John 3:18). As an individual, you either reject or accept the redemption God has provided. To reject the God of redemption puts you on the path of destruction. However, you must keep in mind that it is your own choice which places you on that path, not God's. God's choice for you was life in Jesus Christ, and scripture assures us that when we choose Christ, we choose life!

Theologians have appealed to certain scriptures to support their theology that God will punish sinners. In dealing with the text of those scriptures, it is my intention to show that religious theology has violated God's claim to holiness and has begun to tamper with the biblical text.

"Children of Wrath"

Theologians have translated the Ephesians 2:3 phrase *"children of wrath"*—or the parallel *"vessels of wrath"* in Romans 9:22—as indicating that humanity is the object of God's anger. In the New International Version, Ephesians 2:3 reads, *"We were by nature objects of wrath"* (NIV). The Amplified Bible's translation of this verse inserts God's name into the phrase, making it read *"children of [God's] wrath"* (AMP). It is my intention to show that this is a scandalous violation of the text.

In Ephesians 2, Paul does not introduce God until verse four. Paul then very emphatically and deliberately introduces God with the word "but." By the use of this "but," Paul's intention is to contrast and distance God and his action from any and all action referred to in verses one, two, and three. God is not part of the discussion or under consideration in the first three verses of Ephesians 2.

The subject matter of Ephesians 2:1–3 is the sinful state of human beings. In verse one, this state is referred to as *"dead in trespasses and sins."* In verses two and three, Paul continues to describe this state of death. Obviously, God is not the author or originator of this state of death. Death is the result of refusing to accept the life-giving alternative that God has provided. Paul presents God as the one who loved those in the state of death, and because of that love provided a means of escape from this state and its consequences.

According to Paul's statement, the sinner is already dead, or spiritually without life. Outside the mercy and grace of God, the sinner has no vital signs which give any indication that there is life. Therefore, theologians who hold Ephesians 1:3 as stating that God will punish the sinner are suggesting that God will make sure these people are punished for being in a state of death. This is not consistent with the message of the gospel. Jesus did not come to ensure sinners would be punished for being dead. He came to bring abundant life for everyone.

Beginning with verse two, Paul describes our conduct while in the state of death. As dead people, Paul tells us that we *"walked according to the course of this world, according to the prince of the power of the air."* Paul attributes a person's conduct while in the state of death to being spiritually influenced by the world and Satan. After describing this conduct and who that conduct is associated with, Paul gives this kind of person a descriptive idiomatic title: *"sons of disobedience."*

In verse three, Paul continues to describe this state of death. Unlike verse two, Paul does not focus on who or what this conduct is related to. Instead, he now focuses on the responsibility of the individual for his or her own behaviour. The sinner's behaviour contributes to one's state of death and, as the result, is of one's own *"lusts of our flesh"* (Ephesians 2:3). These lustful pursuits cause the sinner to fulfill *"the desires of the flesh and of the mind"* (Ephesians 2:3). Paul attributes these conditions and actions to a person's nature, and that nature has already been designated as being dead. Then, like in verse two, Paul gives this depraved selfish behaviour a descriptive idiomatic title: *"children of wrath."* Like the *"sons of disobedience"* phrase, this too is a phrase that encapsulates the description just given.

Ephesians 2:3, like verses one and two, spells out the sinner's condition. To introduce God into verse three as subject of the word wrath suggests that God is part of the sinner's selfish behaviour. Reading verse three as *"children of [God's] wrath"* is the same as reading verse two as saying *"sons of [God's] disobedience."* Most theologians would see the latter as blasphemous and unthinkable, yet some theologians have developed a doctrine on the basis of the former. This doctrine has caused biblical scholars to tamper with and add to the biblical text. It is an addition that suggests Paul is saying what is not supported by the context of Ephesians 2:1–3.

In the rest of the chapter, Paul's focus is God's love, mercy, and grace toward us. Not once in the entire chapter (or book, for that matter) does Paul even hint at the idea that God is angry with the sinner, or wants to punish the sinner. Therefore, to designate God as the agent of wrath is to destroy the solidarity of Paul's description of those in the state of death.

Ephesians 2:2–3 are parallel verses; together, they define the state of death referred to in verse one. The phrases *"sons of disobedience"* and *"children of wrath"* are Semitic idioms. These idioms indicate that the characterizations of *wrath* and *disobedience* are original and innate to the individual who is in the state of death.[8] *"Sons of disobedience"* refers to the people who walk according to the course of this world and who are influenced by Satan. *"Children of wrath"* refers to these same people, and the word "wrath" characterizes them as being driven by their own selfish, lustful desires. Both are title phrases that reference the disposition and characteristic behaviour of those who are *"dead in trespasses and sins."* The phrase *"children of wrath"* does not define how God views or relates to such a person. Instead, it describes the character and desires that drive the person who is in the state of death.

Paul designates the Ephesians' former sinful condition as a singular state: *"dead in trespasses and sins."* This singular state of death is described in two ways. First, Paul tells us to whom that state of death is related, followed by a descriptive idiomatic title. Secondly, Paul characterizes the behaviour of those in the state of death and gives that behaviour a descriptive idiomatic title. Reading God into verse three, as the subject of wrath, with the sinner as the

---

[8] Barth, p. 215.

object of that wrath, distorts and violates the intended solidarity of the text.

This violation introduces God into a text that deals exclusively with the sinner's state of death. Paul has deliberately placed the title phrase in juxtaposition (parallel or alongside) to its description. *"Sons of disobedience"* is defined as: 1) walking according to the course of this world, and 2) walking according to the prince of the power of the air. The phrase *"children of wrath"* designates and defines those who are driven to fulfill the desires of: 1) the flesh, and 2) the mind. Paul thereby indicates that a sinner's personal desires give rise to conduct that is driven by wrath. To read God into the phrase *"children of wrath"* is as scandalous as reading the parallel idiomatic phrase as children of God's disobedience.

Reading God into verse three totally ignores the textual "but" of verse four, thereby distorting the contrast and separation Paul intended to make between our condition and God's redemption. As argued above, the revelation of God's wrath provided humanity with redemption from our state of death. In contrast to our action and condition, God as subject of this redemption is introduced in verse four. God's action is presented as that which freed the Ephesians from their former relationships, dispositions, and characteristics. Paul's intention in Ephesians 2:1–3 is to show us our utterly hopeless condition. Without the rich mercy, great love, and grace of God, humans would have been confined to death, given to disobedience and following their own desires and passions that fight and war against God. It is a state in which there is no hope or future.

Ephesians 2:3, like the verse that precedes it, is a description of a person's condition, conduct, and behaviour while in the state of death. If we accept that the idiomatic title phrase in verse two encapsulates the description given in verse two, it logically follows that the idiomatic title phrase of verse three also encapsulates the description given in verse three. Paul has thereby defined and characterized the human condition of death. It is a condition in which a person is under the influence of Satan, given to disobedience, and fulfilling the lusts of the flesh—a condition that Paul characterized as being in conflict with God's will for all of humanity.

In Ephesians 2:3, Paul does not refer to humanity as objects of God's wrath. God's wrath was revealed to redeem humanity, not to destroy humanity. In Ephesians 2, Paul clearly and deliberately separates God and His action from humanity's state, condition, and behaviour. Paul's point is that in spite of our condition, God's mercy and grace is extended to us in order that we might become vessels of that mercy and grace. To reject that mercy and grace is to choose to be a child of wrath who follows and fulfills the desires of one's lustful mind.

Through Jesus Christ, God chose humans to be vessels of his mercy and grace. In Ephesians, Paul states that this choice was made by God before he created the world. God does not hate you. God will not destroy you. In Jesus Christ's death on the cross, God has committed himself to redeem you. In Christ, he has done everything he can to provide salvation for you. Now the choice is yours. You must choose whom you will serve, and that choice determines your quality of life and your destiny.

"Vessels of Wrath"

In Romans 9:22, *"vessels of wrath"* is in the same category as *"children of wrath." "Vessels of wrath"* is a descriptive title designating a person in their *unregenerate* state. *"Vessels of mercy"* (Romans 9:23) is also a descriptive title designating a person in their *regenerate* state. As in Ephesians, Paul's primary focus in this context is God's mercy (note verses 14–16)! Due to God's sovereignty, it is his prerogative to show mercy as he wills. In regard to those who are hardened, Paul makes it very clear that such a one cannot fault God for their condition (Romans 9:20). To support his position, Paul appeals to the analogy of the potter. Because Paul used this analogy, some theologians have concluded that Paul was saying some people are created by God to be vessels of his destructive wrath. Such a conclusion violates Paul's intended use of the analogy, and it violates God's claim to holiness. It is a violation which characterizes God as a Dr. Jekyll and Mr. Hyde.

Paul's appeal to the analogy of the potter is intended to accent and showcase the primary theme of this passage, which is God's mercy and grace. The potter has the right to remake a vessel if it becomes marred. As children of wrath and vessels of wrath, we do not merit God's mercy. Yet God as the potter does not destroy or discard that which became marred in his hand. God remakes the vessel (compare this to 2 Corinthians 5:17).

In Romans 9:22, Paul shows that God's action goes beyond that of a potter. Like in Ephesians 2:4, Paul begins verse 22 with a very significant "but." Cranfield states that this "but" indicates "an element of opposition and implies that he regards his illustration as inadequate."[9] By his use of this "but" in the analogy, Paul "brings out the fact that God's ways are not like a potter's."[10] God is not a potter who arbitrarily creates one vessel for honour and another for dishonour. God, unlike the potter, made it possible for the vessels of wrath (i.e. the children of wrath, those given to following the lust of the flesh and mind) to become vessels of mercy.

It is the vessels of mercy that capture Paul's interest in this context. Paul does not expand further on the vessels of wrath.[11] The statement regarding the vessels of mercy is dominant. The other clauses support and flow into it.[12] Paul is declaring that God's wrath is shown and his power are made known by his endurance and longsuffering of the vessels of wrath, so that he might make known the riches of his glory upon them when they become vessels of mercy. God's intention and purpose is to redeem humanity from its state of death, because that state is demeaning, destructive, and satanically driven.

---

[9] Cranfield, p. 239.
[10] Ibid., p. 239.
[11] Morris, p. 369.
[12] Cranfield, p. 240.

Paul does not indicate that God is the active agent in regards to the vessels of wrath. Like in Ephesians, the emphasis here is on God as agent and initiator of grace, mercy, and hope. And very clearly Paul states that God's wrath is shown through his *"endurance with much longsuffering"* of the vessels of wrath (Romans 9:22). God can't be faulted for what we are by nature. As sinful humans, we are *"children of wrath"* or *"vessels of wrath"* when we follow and give ourselves to lustful desires of the flesh and mind. God can't be blamed for this condition (Romans 9:20). This is especially true in light of the fact that God, like a potter, can take the vessel that became marred and remake it. God has made it possible and is waiting for these vessels of wrath to become vessels of mercy. God has made his choice, so we either choose with him or against him!

If Paul is teaching that God makes some humans for his destructive wrath, then Paul has characterized God as a dysfunctional father. However, Paul presents God as the redeemer who is actively involved in the life and well-being of the vessels of mercy. Paul never uses the verb form of wrath with God as subject. Paul repeatedly uses the verb forms of love, mercy, and grace with God as subject.[13]

Theologians have argued the pros and cons of whether we should see the word "fitted"—in the clause *"fitted for*

---

[13] Dodd, p. 21f. Although Dodd made this point many years ago, theologians appeared to ignore it and continued developing the theology that God will punish the sinner.

destruction" of verse 22—as active or middle voice,[14] but the bottom line is that sin is like an avalanche; it destroys. Those who choose to continue to live in the avalanche zone have thereby rejected the safe haven that has been provided for them. Therefore, they have "fitted" themselves for destruction. It is not logical to assume that the one who provided that safe haven is responsible for the destruction of those who refuse the safe haven. Those who refuse the safe haven fit themselves for destruction because of their refusal of that which was provided.

It should be noted that God's wrath is coupled with his power in Romans 9:22. To see God's wrath and power demonstrated in his destruction of the sinner is not a very fitting demonstration of divine power. In our world, anyone is capable of using power to corrupt and destroy. If destruction was God's will and intention for humanity, why did he send us Jesus? Is destruction the kind of wrath and power we expect to be revealed from heaven? If God is the active agent of both the vessels of wrath and the vessels of mercy, God's kingdom is divided.

On the contrary, God demonstrates his wrath and power by the endurance and longsuffering of sinners. God does not wish or want to see us destroy ourselves. How-

---

[14] The form of the Greek word used can be seen as either. The active voice usually indicates the subject is being acted upon, i.e. the vessel is destined for destruction by another. The middle voice suggests it is the vessel itself that has fitted itself for destruction. I hold it to be middle voice. But even if it is the active voice, Paul does not specify God as the agent that prepares the vessels of wrath for destruction. Given Ephesians 2:2, it is obvious that Satan is the agent of influence in the case of the sons of disobedience.

ever, at the same time, God does not force anyone to move out of the avalanche area. God gives everyone an extended opportunity to repent and turn from their rebellious, self-destructive choices and actions in order that they might know his rich mercy. That is passion and power, indeed!

So when we read about the wrath of God abiding on the unbeliever, as in John 3:36, we need to see it in the light of Romans 9:22. God's wrath abides on the unbeliever because God's intentions, purposes, and plans are to redeem sinners. And since God is holy, the redemption of the sinner is his primary concern and focus. Jesus did not die on the cross in order to make a case against humanity. Jesus died on the cross in order to bring sin to an end in the kingdom of God.

In Ephesians 2:3, Paul defines wrath as fulfilling one's own desires or will. What is God's will and desire? According to 2 Peter 3:9, God's will is that none perish. This being the case, would God's wrath not cause him to strive for his will to be accomplished? Scripture very clearly indicates that God did not send his Son into the world to condemn the world, but to save the world (John 3:17). For theologians to suggest that the sinner is the object of God's anger puts the truth of John 3:16–17 in doubt.

6

The Day of Wrath
vs. The Wrath

T he classical references religion has used to support the idea that God is angry with sinful humanity are the passages that speak about *"the wrath to come"* and *"the day of wrath."* The latter phrase appears only once in the New Testament, in Romans 2:5. In the Romans 2:5 passage, Paul speaks of the *"revelation of the righteous judgment of God"* in relationship to *"the day of wrath."* Theologians have come to understand all of the phrases which speak of *"the wrath to come"* in the New Testament to refer to God's wrath. However, on what exegetical principle can it be concluded that *"the wrath to come"* is the same as *"the day of wrath"*? To come to such a conclusion, one must assume that the definite article in each of these phrases refers to God.

Just because each phrase refers to wrath, we should not jump to the conclusion that each refers to God's wrath. In none of the *"wrath to come"* passages is there ever a reference to the righteous judgment of God, as is the case in reference to the day of wrath. Might this indicate that the phrase *"the wrath to come"* refers to something different than *"the day of wrath"*? To answer that question, let us look at the passages in which the phrase *"the wrath to come"* is used.

Matthew 3:7 and Luke 3:7

In Matthew 3:7 and Luke 3:7, John the Baptist warns of *"the wrath to come."* The phrases are precisely the same in both passages and the word wrath has the definite article. "The" indicates that the writers have a specific, definite, and distinguishable type of wrath in mind. Jumping to the conclusion that "the" designates this as God's wrath only clouds the issue. To read "the" as designating God is adding a specific subject to the text which the text does not specify. Both Matthew's and Luke's statements make one thing very clear: if the Pharisees and Sadducees were to respond positively to John's preaching, it would be possible to avoid *"the wrath to come."* On the other hand, a negative response places these persons in a position of experiencing *"the wrath to come."*

To conclude that this passage speaks of a coming wrath of God demands that we read that conclusion into the text. To do so, we have then added to the text to find the meaning of the text.

Romans 5:8–9

Romans 5:8–9 states, *"But God demonstrates His own love toward us, in that while we were still sinners, Christ died for us. Much more then, having now been justified by His blood, we shall be saved from wrath through Him."* A literal rendering of the final phrase of verse nine would be, "We shall be saved by him from the wrath."

In Romans 5:9, like in Matthew 3:7 and Luke 3:7, the word wrath has the definite article. In this verse Paul, like Matthew and Luke, is silent in regards to the subject or agency of "the wrath." What Paul states very emphatically is that it is by God's grace through Jesus Christ that we are saved from "the wrath." Like the passages from Matthew and Luke, Paul indicates that a positive response to the gospel saves us from "the wrath." A negative response to the gospel puts us in danger of "the wrath."

To conclude that this verse is saying Jesus saves us from God's wrath distorts the gospel message. God is not the destroyer, sin is the destroyer! To suggest that Jesus saves us from the judgmental wrath of his father raises questions about the action of a loving, merciful, longsuffering God. It divides the Godhead into two forces pushing in opposite directions. It suggests that God's redemptive purpose is dualistic, not singular and holy. Instead of the cross being God's ultimate act of history, the cross becomes a divine carrot dangled in front of humanity. The ultimate act of history then becomes the unleashing of God's anger against sinners. Such a message compromises the truth of the gospel. Instead of the gospel being a message of hope for those who are perishing, it becomes a message of doom. Instead of Jesus Christ being the one who frees humanity from sin, he becomes the personification of condemnation and judgment for those who are perishing. Surely John wasn't confused when he indicated that Jesus did not come into the world to condemn the world (John 3:17)!

1 Thessalonians 5:9

A parallel passage to Romans 5:9 is 1 Thessalonians 5:9. There, Paul states, *"For God did not appoint us to wrath, but to obtain salvation through our Lord Jesus Christ."* Since this verse has an eschatological setting, theologians have assumed that the wrath referred to is God's future wrath. It is true that Paul deals with eschatology, and because of this he presents some practical and immediate everyday concerns.

Paul's concern for the Thessalonians is that they be prepared for the day of the Lord. Phrases such as "drunken," "of the night," and "of darkness" describe those who are not prepared for the day of the Lord. Those prepared are described by phrases such as "children of the day" and "children of the light." It is because of the coming day of the Lord that Paul appeals to the Thessalonians to live a certain lifestyle. That appeal is based upon a solid theological truth which Paul presents in verse nine. Here is that truth: God has provided and appointed us to salvation. This theological truth is contrasted from that which God has not appointed us to: namely, wrath. So the theological base upon which Paul builds his appeal has two opposing poles. What God has appointed us to is opposed to that which God has not appointed us to. The theological question that demands an answer is this: is God divided on his purposes and plans for humanity? Has God designated some to salvation while reserving others for his destructive anger? Let us look at the passage to find out the answer.

Here is the test of 1 Thessalonians 5:4–8:

> But you, brethren, are not in darkness, so that this Day should overtake you as a thief. You are all sons of light and sons of the day. We are not of the night nor of darkness. Therefore let us not sleep, as others do, but let us watch and be sober. For those who sleep, sleep at night, and those who get drunk are drunk at night. But let us who are of the day be sober, putting on the breastplate of faith and love, and as a helmet the hope of salvation.

It is clear that the appeal has contrasting points. The children of light stand in contrast to the children of darkness. These two groups are clearly stated to be as different as night and day. So the exegetical question that calls for an answer is this: does Paul's doctrinal truth given in verse 9 mirror the appeal of verses 4–8?

It is obvious that what God has appointed us to—salvation—is "mirrored" in verses 4–8 by phrases such as *"sons of light"* and *"sons of the day."* The fact that the positive is mirrored suggests that the negative is also mirrored. If we accept that the passage suggests a mirroring, then the term wrath is mirrored by the children of the night and darkness. This mirroring then suggests that God did not appoint us to be children of darkness, because in being children of darkness we follow our own desires and passions, which are characteristics Paul attributed to those who are children of wrath.

This mirroring very strongly indicates that, like in Ephesians 2:3 or Romans 9:22, Paul uses the word wrath to characterize the unregenerate state. If we insist on carrying out our own will and desires, which is characterized as wrath, we put ourselves on the slippery slopes of rebellion. It is not God who appointed us to follow our own passions and the lusts of the flesh and mind. In Christ Jesus, God has appointed us to salvation. Therefore, Paul is stating that a positive response to Christ and the gospel is our salvation from carrying out our own rebellious wrath, as well as from experiencing the consequences of that wrath.

1 Thessalonians 1:10

1 Thessalonians 1:10, like 5:9, is concerned with our lifestyle. The Thessalonians had turned from idols to serve God. This turning was as the result of deliverance through

Jesus. Here, Paul equates deliverance from idol worship with deliverance from wrath.[15] To see this as deliverance from God's wrath makes deliverance from idol worship a secondary issue. This would then mean that the primary reason for Jesus' death was to deliver us from the wrath of his own father. Did Jesus come to save us from the wrath of his father, or from our own selfish acts, like idol worship? Obviously, Jesus came to save us from our own self-ish acts of sin, acts which result in death and destruction. In 1 Thessalonians 1:10, the sin of idol worship is refer-enced as wrath. Therefore, like the other references con-sidered above, the word wrath is used to characterize the Thessalonians' lustful and selfish personal conduct. The conduct of idol worship is portrayed as an act of wrath against God.

1 Thessalonians 2:15

In 1 Thessalonians 2:16, Paul speaks about the Jewish op-position to the proclamation of the gospel. In verse six-teen, Paul states, "...forbidding us to speak to the Gentiles that they may be saved, always filling up their sins: is come upon them the wrath to the uttermost" (my own literal transliteration of the Greek text).

In Greek grammar, that which is emphasized can stand at the beginning of a sentence or clause. This is true

---

[15] In Acts 19:28, it is recorded that the people of Ephesus responded in wrath when the production of idols was threatened.

for the words *"is come."* Thus Paul's apparent emphasis is that "the wrath" had already overtaken these Jews. There are three other references where the identical form of the verb *"is come"* is used in scripture. Those references are Romans 9:31, Luke 11:20, and Matthew 12:28. In Romans, it is used to indicate that Israel did not attain righteousness by the law. In the two Gospel passages, it is used to indicate that the kingdom of God has come because Jesus cast out devils by the power of God. In each of the three passages, the present indicative of *"is come"* designates that which has happened, and not something yet to come. In these cases, the present indicative is not used as a prophetic future, which is sometimes the case in Greek grammar. There is no evidence that Paul used it as a prophetic future in 1 Thessalonians 2:16. *"Is come"* speaks of that which is and not something yet to happen. Add to this the placement of the word at the beginning of the clause concerning wrath and it must be concluded that Paul was emphasizing the fact that these Jews were experiencing and expressing "the wrath."

It should also be noted that Paul used the definite article with the word wrath. He is therefore speaking of a specific, definite, and distinguishable kind of wrath. Because Paul states "is come upon them the wrath," we should not look beyond them but *at* them to understand what "the wrath" refers to.

These Jews forbade the preaching of the gospel to the Gentiles. In doing so, they, as children of wrath, filled up their sins. This action constitutes being overtaken by the wrath *"to the uttermost."* These Jews, as children and vessels of wrath, were living out the desires of a religious mindset to its fullest extreme. They were withstanding and forbidding the proclamation of the gospel message to the Gentiles. This opposition is characterized by Paul as "the wrath" having overtaken them to the uttermost.

To see this passage as speaking of a future eschatological wrath of God demands that we go into exegetical contortions. God's name must be inserted in place of the definite article, which means we have arbitrarily added to the text to find the meaning of the text. Then, to support this unfounded addition, we must see *"is come"* as a prophetic future while at the same time maintaining that this guarantees that these Jews will experience God's wrath to the full. However, such an understanding ignores Paul's literal words. Paul has deliberately and pointedly indicated that these Jews have filled up their sins by stating that "the wrath is come upon them to the uttermost." It is not God's wrath that is pointed to here; it is the Jewish religious sect's active opposition to the proclamation of the gospel that is being dealt with, and that active opposition is characterized as "the wrath."

These Jews fulfill what John the Baptist warned against: *"the wrath to come."* John's warning did not concern God's wrath but man's bent to follow his own lusts and desires of the flesh. Walking after the spirit of this world brings man to reject Jesus, and in its most extreme expression leads to man actively forbidding the preaching of the gospel. Forbidding the preaching of the gospel is man's wrath taken to its ultimate state.

The above does not address the issue of the "day of wrath" in which Paul states the righteous judgment of God will be revealed. In section three of this book, we turn our attention to the book of Revelation to examine what is meant by the day of wrath and the revelation of God's righteous judgment.

PART
THREE

INTRODUCTION

L ike the religious Jews of Jesus' day, many today believe that God must deal with the evil and wickedness of this world before his kingdom can be established on earth. The final book of the Bible, Revelation, is read and understood as supporting this belief. Theologians who hold to this view of Revelation see it as describing seven years of unparalleled catastrophe. These seven years, commonly called the tribulation, are seen as the transition period between our present age, which is also known as the Church age, and the age to come, or the millennium age. This transitional tribulation period is held to be marked by seven years of crisis, all of which are God ordained and in which humanity cries to be hidden *"from the face of Him who sits on the throne and from the wrath of the Lamb!"* (Revelation 6:16)

For this study, I have chosen to call this view of Revelation "Tribulation Theology." Tribulation Theology holds the Lamb of Revelation to be a dichotomous (divided) symbol. The Lamb is held to be symbolic of redemption during our present Church age, which leads up to the time of transition. However, at the time the tribulation begins, the symbolism of the Lamb changes to a warring ram in order to establish the kingdom of God on earth. As a warring ram, he is intent on a literal physical judgment of those who are on earth.

If this view is the truth presented in Revelation, then biblical Christology—the gospel and the gospel's message about Jesus Christ—must conform to the Tribulation Theology model. This would demand that at some point there is a transformation in the biblical symbolism of the Lamb. Such a transformation would in turn infer that the wrath of God revealed at the cross did not completely appease God's anger against the sinner. In essence, this adds a caveat to the gospel. Tribulation Theology must then explain how Jesus appeased God's anger against the sinner, but only selectively and temporarily. For if the wrath of the Lamb portrays judgment against sin, the atonement for sin by the Lamb is then not an all-sufficient action. And if the Lamb's atonement for sinners is not all-sufficient, how do seven years of tribulation appease God's anger?

These are questions that Tribulation Theology does not deal with. For this reason, Tribulation Theology must be called into question and brought to account. Therefore, the question that concerns us in this section is, is the Lamb of Revelation a dichotomous figure? If so, then Tribulation

Theology has a point. But if the symbolism of the Lamb
does not change into a warring ram, then how should one
understand the references in Revelation to God's wrath
and the Lamb's wrath?

7

John's Vision
of the Lamb

I n Revelation 5, John introduces us to the Lamb. John
is shown a sealed scroll in the hand of the one who sits
on the throne.[16] There is no one found worthy to
break the seals and reveal the contents of the scroll. John
weeps, because he will not realize what the scroll reveals.

---

[16] Tribulation Theology holds to a futuristic view of Revelation. I, however, am more closely aligned with the historicist view, and hold Revelation to be describing the conditions of the world in the Church age.
Thus, the seven sealed scroll speaks of the history of the Church age
marked by seven sequential periods of time. Osborne, in his discussion
of the various views, dismisses the historicist view as having very little
to support it. I beg to differ. What John hears and sees in Revelation 5
argues strongly for a historicist view. However, the purpose of this
book is not a study of the various views and which view best explains
Revelation. Instead, this book is a study of God's wrath and whether or
not the revelation of that wrath is consistent with the gospel as outlined
in Romans 1:16-18. I hold that it must be in order for God's wrath to be
holy. So my study of scripture as it relates to the subject of God's wrath
has moved me away from the Tribulation Theology view into the historicist view and the reader needs to keep this in mind as he or she
reads on.

John is then informed that *"the Lion of the tribe of Judah, the Root of David"* (Revelation 5:5) has overcome sin and is therefore worthy to take the scroll and loose its seven seals. However, after being informed that the Lion is worthy, John does not see a Lion. Instead, he sees a Lamb.

John refers to this Lamb well over thirty times in Revelation.[17] This Lamb is stated to have been slain and has thereby *"redeemed us to God by Your blood out of every tribe and tongue and people and nation"* (Revelation 5:9). Thus, Revelation 5:9 clearly states that the Lamb is worthy to take the scroll and open its seals on the basis of having provided redemption. Therefore, the clearly stated role of the Lamb, when introduced in Revelation 5, is that he is the provider of redemption. The provision of this redemption is what makes him worthy to take the scroll and open its seals. This, in essence, makes the Lamb and redemption one and the same; therefore, it could be said that redemption breaks the seals and allows the historical events that Revelation describes to take place.

In Revelation, this Lamb breaks the seven seals (6:1, 8:1) The Lamb provides white robes for the tribulation saints and is also their shepherd (7:14, 7:17). He is the one who overcomes end-time evil (6:15–17, 12:11, 17:14). The Lamb is the leader of the 144,000 (14:4). In Revelation

---

[17] Osborne speaks of the Lamb being named twenty-nine times (p. 256), but the Lamb is referenced as "he," "you," and "your" five times in Chapter 5, and five times as "he" in relation to opening the seals. Adding these ten personal pronoun references to the twenty-nine times that the Lamb is named, there are thirty-nine references to the Lamb in Revelation.

17:14, the Lamb is declared *"King of kings and Lord of lords."*
In Revelation 19, the Lamb takes a bride. The Lamb is the
temple and light of New Jerusalem (21:22–23), and it is the
Lamb who occupies the throne with God (22:1). Obviously, the Lamb dominates the book of Revelation and
ushers in the kingdom of God. Is this Lamb a redemptive
Lamb, a militaristic ram, or both? That is the question that
demands an answer!

The Lion Transformed into a Lamb

The words of Revelation 5:5 would have had compelling
meaning for John. John was a Jew, raised and educated in
the expectation of a coming Messiah who would reign on
David's throne.[18] The promises of such a Messianic ruler
are given in two Old Testament passages: Genesis 49:9 and
Isaiah 11:1. It is these very verses that are combined in the
words which John hears. For John, as well as the other
disciples of Jesus, these passages elicited a very strong literal Messianic expectation. They believed Jesus to be the
Messianic Lion of the tribe of Judah who would establish
the kingdom of God on earth. They expected Jesus, as the
Messianic Lion, to usher in this kingdom of God. As the
Messiah, Jesus was expected to rule on David's throne, and
that expectation included the deliverance of Israel from

---

[18] It is assumed that John the Apostle is the author of Revelation. Some
Bible scholars debate the authorship of Revelation. If John the Apostle
wasn't the author, the author was still a contemporary of the Apostles
and like the Apostles would have had the same Messianic expectations.

Roman occupation. This Messianic expectation ignited a personal passion for John and his brother James. Together, they request being seated on either side of Jesus in his coming kingdom (Mark 10:35–45). Mark notes that this request gave rise to a storm of jealousy among the rest of the disciples. For this reason, Jesus instructed his disciples concerning such aspirations. In that instruction, Jesus doesn't deny that he is the Messiah, and his not denying it suggests that he ascents to the fact that he is, but who would sit on his right or left was not his decision to make (Mark 10:40).

After Christ's death and resurrection, the disciples' expectation in regard to the establishment of his kingdom is expressed in a very specific question: *"Lord, will You at this time restore the kingdom to Israel?"* (Acts1:6) The disciples no longer had aspirations about who would sit where, but they still had the expectation that Jesus was the promised Messiah, and as the Messiah his mandate was to establish the kingdom of God. For the disciples, the establishment of God's kingdom entailed the reestablishment of Israel as a sovereign nation. So, they ask Jesus a pointed question: "Will you restore the kingdom to Israel?" They asked a specific question and Jesus gave them a specific answer. They would not know—that is, they would not "experience" the restoration of the kingdom of Israel.[19] They were not living in the time or season when Israel would once more become an independent nation. By his answer, Jesus

---

[19] The Greek word for "know" references a literal physical experience (see Luke 1:34).

implied that the reestablishment of Israel as a nation was not the focal point of the establishment of God's kingdom. The two are not synonymous. Instead, what John hears and sees focuses the establishment of the kingdom on a person, and the redemption that this person provided. In Revelation 5:6, that person and action is symbolized by a Lamb, which appears as having been slain.

How John and the disciples understood and/or processed Jesus' words in Acts we are not told. However, fast forward a few decades and we find John hearing the same words that had ignited the passionate desires of his younger years. What would John's thoughts have been upon hearing this Messianic promise in his latter years? Obviously, these words would have reminded him of the expectations and questions of his youth. He had fully expected Jesus Christ to fulfill these eschatological passages. John's expectations were for the establishment of Israel as a ruling nation. What he hadn't been sure about was the timing of that fulfillment. Now, here he is on the Island of Patmos and he is once again brought face to face with the same words that had elicited a very specific eschatological expectation in his younger years. What he hears and sees brings John to a startling realization about the kingdom of God!

The Lamb of the Kingdom

In Revelation 5:5, John is given two commands. The first, *"Do not weep,"* is in reference to his grief, because he wasn't going to realize the content of the scroll. This is immediately followed by a second command: *"Behold."* John is being ordered to pay attention and understand the significance of what he is hearing and what he will be shown at that very moment. In his early years, John had expected a literal fulfillment of the Messianic passages, and for him, at that time, that literal fulfillment required the involvement of Israel as a nation. Now he is being ordered to understand the prophetic text. *"Behold"* calls for him to pay explicit attention and not allow the prophetic text to be sidetracked by his former expectations.

Was he being ordered to understand the promise differently than he had in his younger years? Surely he wasn't wrong about Jesus being the *"lion of the tribe of Judah."* True, Jesus hadn't restored Israel to its former glory and national status, and John had been told he wasn't going to experience that restoration. So he had been wrong about seeing the nation of Israel as being vital to the establishment of God's kingdom. Were there other parts of his expectations that were not realistic?

John's next words—*"And I looked"*—focus our attention on a portrait that leaps out of the text. By saying *"I looked,"* John indicates that he was obedient to the commands given to him. The first command was to stop weeping. Tears distort and obstruct clear vision! John is absolutely sure of what he saw. John's *"I looked"* indicates that his vision was unobstructed. But even more importantly, *"I looked"* indicates that what he saw is the key to understanding the Old Testament Messianic text. No longer is his understanding of the passages based on his traditional

Jewish eschatological expectations. The Old Testament's proclamations are transformed into visual reality. This visual reality is like the proverbial picture, and it truly is worth a thousand words.

The second command, *"Behold,"* indicates that the Lamb fulfills the promises of the Messianic texts! The Messianic promise is presented in an up to the minute living portrait. The Lamb is the embodiment and fulfillment of the Old Testament's eschatological Messianic promises. The Lion is transformed into a Lamb! The establishment of the kingdom is centered in the Lamb, the redeemer of Israel and the world. John is shown that a kingdom is defined by its King. God's kingdom is defined by the Lamb that was slain! God's kingdom is established by and through redemption. Note it and never forget it! It is through the redemption of sinners that God's kingdom comes into being. God's kingdom does not become established by the destruction or the overthrow of evil people or evil nations.

John follows his *"I looked"* with the imperative *"Behold."* John uses the same word as used by the elder who addressed him. Undoubtedly, John is using the word to draw our attention to a very important point. He is passing on the command to the reader. The reader is ordered to understand and comprehend the significance of what he heard and then saw, just like John himself had been ordered to pay attention and understand.

John takes what he hears and sees beyond the realm of "beautiful mixed metaphors."[20] This second *"Behold"* indicates that John is taken by surprise at the profound truth inherent in what he sees. This indicates that John understands, and wants us to understand, that the Lamb fulfills the role of the Old Testament's prophetic Messianic Lion. John had expected the Messiah to deal physically and decisively with the Romans and bring their occupation of Israel to an end. However, Jesus as the Lion did not crush the occupational rule of the barbaric Romans. Instead, Jesus as the Lion of the tribe of Judah suffered a cruel crucifixion as a Lamb. Jesus did so in order to be the redeemer and thereby establish a kingdom for both Jews and Gentiles. In God's kingdom, a Lamb sits on the throne, and he is seated there right now. So God's kingdom is unlike any other kingdom in this world.

John's *"behold"* indicates that the Lamb fulfills the role of the prophetic Lion. As the Lamb, Jesus provided redemption. And without redemption there can be no rebirth, which is the prerequisite for seeing the kingdom of God (John 3:3). The realization of the eschatological kingdom is not brought about by the exaltation of one nation over another. God's kingdom is not realized through the destruction of a sinful nation or the destruction of sinful people. God's kingdom is realized by being born into it. God's kingdom comes into reality in and through redeemed people following their leader: the Lamb. The redeeming Lamb is declared *"King of kings and Lord of lords"*

---

[20] Osborne, p. 254.

(Revelation 17:14). God's kingdom is established through the leadership of the overcoming Lamb, and without the redeeming Lamb there is no possibility of a kingdom. Without the redemptive Lamb, eschatology cannot be realized. It is only the redemptive Lamb that is worthy to break the seals.

All kingdoms rise or fall on the basis of who is in charge. In the kingdom of God, it is the Lamb who is in charge. Those who follow the Lamb help establish his kingdom. Those who reject the Lamb reject the king of God's kingdom.

John's experience, as recorded in Revelation 5, makes it very clear that without the Lamb, eschatology—the future Messianic kingdom—cannot be realized. Revelation unfolds under the jurisdiction and administration of the Lamb. Only the Lamb can bring the kingdom of God into reality. The Lion of the tribe of Judah is not seen or mentioned again throughout the rest of Revelation, whereas the Lamb is repeatedly referenced, indicating that the Lion's role is indeed fulfilled by the Lamb.

The Paschal Lamb

A question of vital importance to our study of God's wrath is, who is this Lamb that John sees? Our answer to this question determines how we view the role of God's wrath and the wrath of the Lamb in fulfilling the events described in Revelation. Since Revelation is concerned with eschatology, how we view the Lamb's wrath determines our view of how that eschatology is realized.

In John 1:29–35, it is Jesus who is declared the Lamb of God who takes away the sin of the world. In Revelation 1:5, John identifies Jesus Christ as the person who shed his blood for our sins. In Revelation 5:6, John speaks of this Lamb *"as though it had been slain."* Osborne indicates that John is applying Isaiah's "Suffering Servant of Yahweh" to Jesus Christ.[21] However, in Revelation, John uses the Greek term *arnion* rather than *amnos*, as used in his gospel, when John names the Lamb as the one who takes away the sin of the world. Thus, *amnos* is used to designate Jesus as the Lamb before his death. *Arnion* is the term used by John in Revelation. Why?

Arnion carries with it a sense of endearment. Jesus uses the term *arnion* when he tells Peter, *"Feed My lambs"* (John 21:15). In Revelation, John adopts this endearing term to designate Jesus as the Lamb. Osborne states of the term that it "combines the images of the Passover lamb of Exodus and the Suffering Servant lamb of Isaiah."[22]

It needs to be noted that *arnion* is an exclusive use of the term for the Lamb in Revelation. John uses no other term for the Lamb, even when he speaks of the beast in Revelation 13:11 as having *"two horns like a lamb."* This exclusive use would suggest that John is intending to convey a symbolic understanding that is specific and consistent throughout the narrative.

---

[21] Ibid., p. 255.
[22] Ibid., p. 256.

In Revelation 5:6, John speaks of the Lamb *"as though it had been slain."* This fact is reiterated in 5:9, and stated for the third time in 5:12. In 5:9, his sacrifice is clearly stated to have provided redemption through his blood. Thus in Revelation 5, where John introduces us to this endearing Lamb, there is no doubt that the Lamb (*arnion*) is symbolic of redemption. If this is true for the entire book of Revelation, then John's exclusive use of *arnion* would indicate that he is referencing the redemption provided by that Lamb every time he uses the term.

In Revelation 7:9–10, the great multitude from all nations ascribes salvation to the Lamb. In Revelation 7:14, this great multitude is referenced as the tribulation saints and are said to have *"washed their robes and made them white in the blood of the Lamb."* In Revelation 12:11, the saints are said to overcome Satan *"by the blood of the Lamb."* Revelation 13:8 speaks of *"the Book of Life of the Lamb slain from the foundation of the world."* In Revelation 14:4, the 144,000 are referenced as *"these were redeemed from among men, being firstfruits to God and to the Lamb."* These verses clearly indicate that when the Lamb is named, that name is associated with Jesus Christ's sacrifice and redemptive work on the cross. In Revelation 5, where John introduces the Lamb, this is definitely the case. Not once in any of the verses where the term *arnion* is used does John hint at the possibility that he is referencing any other action or symbolism for the Lamb. Redemption is clearly the one and only stated action associated with the word *arnion*. Therefore, each repeated use of *arnion* carries with it the redemptive work ascribed to him in Chapter 5. John's exclusive use of *arnion* strongly indicates that, unless there is clear evidence to the contrary, all uses of the term must be understood to be symbolic of and referencing the atoning work of Jesus Christ.

Tribulation Theology does not understand or present the term *arnion* as an exclusive symbol for redemption. In Tribulation Theology, the Lamb of Revelation is a dichotomous figure. For example, Grant R. Osborne presents a strong case for the Lion being transformed into the redemptive Lamb.[23] And that, indeed, is what John associates the Lamb with, as shown above. However, Osborne also argues that this redemptive Lamb is further transformed into a conquering ram, and that this eschatological ram symbolism dominates the Book.[24] He dismisses those who support a singular symbolism—the redemptive paschal Lamb—by stating that the transformation to the militaristic conquering ram is present in the "seven horns" imagery.[25] For this reason, theologians like Osborne present the Lamb as having "two aspects, the sacrificial Lamb and the military ram" who holds forth God's mercy and

---

[23] Ibid., pp. 254-255. In his introduction to his book, Osborne states, "It is clear that the sacrifice of Jesus as the slain Lamb is the key theme" (p. 35).

[24] Ibid., pp. 255-256. Osborne states, "Jesus is the 'slain Lamb' who triumphs and becomes the eschatological Ram" (p. 35). He further states, "These two aspects—slain Lamb and eschatological Ram—dominate the book." l do not classify Osborne as espousing Tribulation Theology, but his futuristic leanings (p. 21) give it support.

[25] Osborne states, "The ram image is introduced in the 'seven horns' of verse 6b. It is part of the transformation techniques used in verses 5-6 from the lion to the lamb to the slain lamb to the conquering ram" (p. 256).

justice.[26] Although Osborne doesn't specifically state what he means by the term "justice," it appears that he agrees with the Tribulation Theology model.

So the question that will be dealt with in the next chapter is, do the seven horns change the symbolic Lamb into a militaristic ram? If the seven horns do not change the symbolism of the Lamb, then Tribulation Theology must be prepared to defend its theology or acknowledge its error concerning the symbolism of the Lamb and its horns.

---

[26] Osborne states, "In short, in Revelation the Lamb of God has two aspects, the sacrificial lamb and the military ram, and they are interconnected, standing at the heart of the book and depicting the two sides of God's activity, his mercy and his justice" (p. 256).

8

The Lamb: A Redeemer, Not a Militaristic Ram

Osborne's exegesis on the seven horns of the Lamb raises a number of questions. The first question we need to consider is, does the animal determine the nature and purpose of its horns, or do the horns determine the nature and action of the animal? Osborne's argument supports the position that the horns determine the nature and action of the animal.

If horns determine the nature of the animal, then the second beast of Revelation 13:11 is truly lamb-like, in that it carries two horns like the Lamb's. But do the lamb-like horns change the beast into a lamb? Definitely not! John states of this beast that *"he had two horns like a lamb and spoke like a dragon"* (Revelation 13:11). Therefore, to argue that the lamb-like horns change the beast's symbolism is unreasonable. Such a position is clearly not supported by the text of Revelation. The beast of Revelation 13 is clearly the antitype of the Lamb. The beast is a deceiver and a fraud and it is his lamb-like horns that testify to that fact. The two lamb-like horns serve to emphasize that this beast is up to no good, even though he appears to be adopting lamb-like tendencies.

In contrast, the Lamb is a redeemer, and his seven horns testify to that fact. Proper exegesis demands that the animal determines the nature of its horns and that the seven horns give further testimony to the nature and symbolism of the Lamb.

The Lamb Is the Primary Symbol

There is also a second problem with seeing the seven horns as designating the Lamb as a warring ram. The Lamb is obviously a primary symbol, while the horns are a secondary symbol. How can this secondary symbolism turn a primary symbol into a different primary symbol?

First and foremost, without the Lamb there is no one to break the seven seals, and therefore no possibility of further revelation. Without the Lamb, John could not have seen or heard what followed. Secondly, it has already been noted that the term *arnion* is exclusively used to designate the Lamb. When John associates *arnion* with any activity, he associates the Lamb with redemption. This association is also exclusive. Not once does John associate the Lamb with any militaristic action. If the horns change the primary symbolism of the Lamb into a militaristic ram, it would be expected that this would be indicated in the text.

In the entire book of Revelation, the Lamb's horns are only noted twice—once in Revelation 5:6 and once in Revelation 13:11, where the beast is said to have two horns, like a lamb. This limited mention of the horns suggests the horns are definitely a secondary symbol, and this secondary symbolism does not change the beast's primary symbolism. The administrative role of the Lamb and the repeated references to him, by name, indicate that the Lamb is a primary symbol that stands in contrast to the beast.

Osborne's exegesis suggests that this primary symbolism of the Lamb, which is textually associated with redemption throughout the narrative, is altered and transformed into a warring ram by a singular mention of the Lamb's seven horns. Therefore, Osborne's exegesis implies that the secondary symbolism of horns, which is only mentioned one time, overrides the clear and repeatedly stated association between the Lamb and redemption. Osborne's exegesis implies that secondary symbols take precedence over textual statements and primary symbols. If this is true for a primary symbol, how can we be sure about any symbolic meaning for any term in Revelation? The Lamb's symbolism in the text is too important to the text to be left to speculation.

Osborne is correct in seeing the Lion as being transformed into the paschal Lamb. Both the Lion and Lamb are primary symbols. The Lion is the Messianic symbol of the Old Testament. According to our understanding of

Old Testament eschatology, this Messianic Lion would establish the kingdom of God. John sees the Lamb as the New Testament fulfillment of the promised Old Testament Messiah. As the Lamb, Jesus ushered in the kingdom of God as a reality on the earth. The transformation of the Lion into the Lamb indicates that a primary Old Testament symbol is transformed and given fulfillment of meaning by a New Testament primary symbol. Even Osborne presents the Lamb as the final stage of that transformation.[27]

So where is the clear scriptural evidence indicating that the primary symbolism of the Lamb is in turn changed into a militaristic ram? In order for this to be true, John would have had to introduce the lamb as a ram, either by another symbolic transformation or by stating that the horns change the Lamb into a symbolic militaristic ram. John does not do so!

Appealing to Old Testament scriptures regarding the symbolism of ram horns and then applying that Old Testament symbolism to the word as used by John is like pouring new wine into old wineskins. It destroys the Old and New Testaments' right to use symbolism as distinctive to their particular message and purpose.

Since John only associates the Lamb with redemption, that singular symbolic understanding becomes paramount to the understanding of the text. John's endearing term for the Lamb is not used in the Old Testament. It is a term

---

[27] Osborne states, "The direction of the transformation is very important; the final stage is the lamb, not the lion" (p. 254).

that is distinctly New Testament in language and usage. To argue that the seven horns transform this endearing, redemptive Lamb into a militaristic ram gives greater weight to symbolism drawn from Old Testament texts instead of allowing John to establish the Lamb as having a clearly distinct New Testament symbolism.

John was definitively instructed to write what he saw in a book *"and send it to the seven churches which are in Asia"* (Revelation 1:11). Revelation is a New Testament book. As the last book of the New Testament, it is the final word on the gospel writings, and the redemptive Lamb dominates the book! This clearly implies that, like the rest of the gospel message, Revelation establishes that the fulfillment of the Old Testament's covenant, predictions, and promises are realized in the Lamb.

What John hears and sees clearly indicates that the Old Testament symbolism of the Lion is transformed and fulfilled in the Lamb. This makes the transformation from Lion to Lamb a precedent-setting transformation. Given this transformation, we would expect the same, or something similar, in order to see the symbolism of the Lamb transformed further into a warring ram. Without such a symbolic transformation or statement to that effect, Osborne's exegesis must be questioned.

Proper exegesis calls for the primary symbol to give meaning to the secondary symbol, unless otherwise stated. This is obviously the case in Revelation 13. The beast is the primary symbol. Even though this beast has lamb-like horns, that alone cannot change the primary symbolism of the beast. The beast is a deceiver and the lamb-like horns suggest he uses lamb-like characteristics to deceive. He has two lamb-like horns, but he speaks *"like a dragon"* (Revelation 13:11). The mention of the lamb-like horns suggests that the beast uses two lamb-like characteristics to deceive. If the lamb-like horns symbolize a militaristic ram, it would suggest that the beast of Revelation 13 tries to deceive with militaristic ram-like characteristics. However, the text implies that the Lamb and his horns stand in direct contrast to the beast. So the Lamb and his horns testify of symbolism that is in keeping with the significance and meaning inherent in the Lamb as a redeemer.

Concerning the symbolism of the Lamb's seven horns, John states in Revelation 5:6 that they are symbolic of *"the seven Spirits of God."* In stating this, John is declaring that the horns, like the eyes, have a specified symbolism. The horns are symbolic of the seven Spirits of God. Osborne observes that *"the eyes are further identified as the [seven] spirits of God."*[28] By not including the horns in this statement, he implies that the horns are not included in this identity. To see the phrase *"which are the seven Spirits of God"* as only referencing the eyes suggests that the horns stand alone without a textual designation or identity. Without such a textual identity, the horns then have no stated symbolic significance or relevance. Without such an identity or reference, stating that they represent the horns of a militaristic ram is an arbitrary assumption. This assumption must then be read into the text. On the contrary, we must accept that the word *"which"* references both the eyes and

---

[28] Ibid., p. 257.

the horns as symbolic of the seven Spirits of God. By designating the eyes and horns as the seven Spirits of God, John has given a New Testament symbolic meaning to the seven horns, just like the seven eyes. It would then follow that John's statement concerning the horns and eyes further expands on the Lamb's designated redemptive portfolio.

Let us consider the meaning inherent in what John hears and sees. John hears the Old Testament promise of a Lion-like Messianic deliverer. The words he hears would have brought all of his former Messianic expectations to mind. John obviously would have expected that he would now become more fully informed regarding the Messianic promise. Then, as he turns, he sees the Lamb as though slain. The transformation from the stated Old Testament deliverer to a visible New Testament symbolism is a very clear and strong indication that what is seen fulfills what is heard. Therefore, the paschal Lamb, Jesus as Redeemer, is the key to the fulfillment of eschatology, and is therefore the key to ushering in the kingdom of God. Redemption makes it possible for the seals to be broken. Redemption allows for history to continue. Christ's atonement for the sins of the world becomes the means by which the age of grace becomes reality, as well as the means by which we can experience the kingdom of God.

Redemption and everything it entails is depicted as having seven eyes and seven horns. The number seven suggests perfection. Eyes designate sight, and by extension knowledge and wisdom. The seven eyes therefore suggest perfect knowledge and wisdom or, as Osborne states, "omniscience."[29] Horns speak of power and ability, and therefore a symbol of the Lamb's perfect omnipotent power.[30] Redemption is God's perfect omniscient and omnipotent plan for bringing the kingdom of God into reality on earth and for delivering the world from bondage to sin, death, and destruction. Or, as Paul indicates, the preaching of Christ crucified is *"the power of God and the wisdom of God"* (1 Corinthians 1:24). John was unable to find anyone on earth, in heaven, or under the earth who was worthy to take the scroll and break the seals, which indicates that without the redemptive Lamb the kingdom of God cannot be realized!

Tribulation Theology, like Jewish eschatology, holds that the Lamb's work of redemption is not sufficient for bringing about the reality of God's kingdom. Both God's and the Lamb's wrath are presented as warring against the individual and corporate sins of the world in order to establish the kingdom of God. This suggests that the Lamb's sacrifice did not fulfill God's requirements for atonement, nor did the Lamb's sacrifice totally appease God's anger against sin. To see the Lamb as a warring ram suggests that, in order for redemption to be completed and ratified, God and the Lamb must literally and physically punish sin and the sinner. However, such reasoning takes away the glory of the cross and the gospel. The gospel message is clear. There is only one person and one event that meets

---

[29] Ibid., p. 257. Omniscience is a tem meaning "all knowing."
[30] Ibid., p. 257. Omnipotence is a term meaning "all powerful."

God's requirements and thereby atoned for sin. That person is the Lamb, and that event is the cross!

In God's kingdom, the problem of sin has been dealt with. In the sacrifice of the Lamb, ungodliness and unrighteousness have been dealt with once and for all. The Lamb made an end of sin! There is no other event or person that can satisfy God's demand for justice and righteousness. As John emphatically declares, he found no other who was worthy to break the seals. If the Lamb's death on the cross isn't an adequate sacrifice for our sin, how can seven years of tribulation, anyone else, or anything else appease God's anger against sin and the sinner?

9

The Opening of the Seals and the Wrath of the Redemptive Lamb

Tribulation Theology presents John's references to God's and the Lamb's wrath in Revelation as pointing to God's punishment of the sinner. This position appears to drive its interpretation and fictional presentations of Revelation. However, it is clear that Revelation 5, which introduces the Lamb, says nothing about the judgment of sinners. Revelation 5:9 states:

> And they sang a new song, saying:
> "You are worthy to take the scroll,
> And to open its seals;
> For You were slain,
> And have redeemed us to God by your
>   blood
> Out of every tribe and tongue and people
>   and nation."

This scripture clearly states that the Lamb is the redeemer of sinners. It is because the Lamb provided this redemption that he is declared worthy to take the scroll and open the seven seals. It is the redemptive Lamb who is given the administrative portfolio of Revelation, and without him the events that follow could not take place.

It is redemption that causes the *"ten thousand times ten thousand"* (Revelation 5:11) in the throne room to erupt into overwhelming adoration and worship of the Lamb. In Revelation 5, the Lamb is worshipped as the redeemer without reservation. It is established that the future events described in Revelation 6 and following are under the jurisdiction of the redemptive Lamb. Without this redemptive Lamb, each successive seal could not be opened. But when this one and only hero of Revelation 5 opens the first and each subsequent seal, the action that breaks forth stands in stark contrast to the overwhelming worship and honour given to him in Revelation 5.

What is happening, and why is it happening? Why such overwhelming worship in heaven, as recorded in Revelation 5, but not even a hint of worship on earth, when this redemptive Lamb carries out his mandated portfolio?

As the Lamb breaks the first four seals, four horsemen burst onto the scene in quick succession. None of these horsemen give the slightest hint of recognition or acknowledgement of the Lamb. These horsemen burst forth as if they are mandated to usher in their own agenda. How is it that in the throne room the Lamb is recognized, worshipped, and given an administrative portfolio for what he accomplished, but when the Lamb carries out his designated mission and portfolio he isn't even acknowledged? Is this indicative of the contrast between what happens in heaven and what happens on earth? Jesus taught us to pray, *"Your kingdom come. Your will be done on earth as it is in heaven"* (Matthew 6:10).

John was told to write and send this letter to the seven churches of Asia. Those churches were called to fervency and service to their Lord. Did the situation in the seven churches deteriorate to such an extent that the Church failed? Clearly the Church's redeemer and Lord is obviously present and carrying out his portfolio. Does no one on earth recognize him? The Lamb as redeemer and Lord is present and active! Where is the Church? Why isn't she seen worshipping the Lamb? Did she, like Jesus' disciples at his arrest, desert him and flee?

As the Lamb carries out his designated task, there isn't a hint of worship. God's redemptive intentions, plans, and purposes appear to be trampled underfoot by horse and rider. Redemption, symbolized by the Lamb, isn't recognized, considered, or acknowledged by the horsemen. The four horsemen that burst forth are intent on their own agenda. They don't stop to thank or even acknowledge the Lamb who made it possible for them to appear on the stage of Revelation's history. Instead of the situation getting better with the breaking of each successive seal, man's inhumanity towards man increases and becomes more and more degenerative and barbaric. The lack of recognition and acknowledgement of the Lamb leads humanity into ever deeper self-destructive action. The description, given

by John, after each seal is opened is like Paul's description
in Ephesians 2:3—children of wrath fulfilling the desires of
the flesh and mind.

Even the four living creatures, the worship leaders in
Revelation 4 and 5, appear to be muted and paralyzed by
the escalation of evil that breaks forth. Their command-
like shouts to "come and see" are like astonished exclama-
tions of unbelieving shock and horror. Incredibly, their
hero—the Lamb—is ignored. The fanatic activity that
erupts with the breaking of each seal seems to slam all
doors to the worship of the Lamb. The horsemen burst
forth completely intoxicated with their own agenda and
mission. God's perfect omniscient and omnipotent plan for
bringing his kingdom into reality on earth is swept aside.
The Lamb who came to make the kingdom of God a reality on earth is ignored and rejected. His redemptive purpose is replaced by the horsemen's aspirations, actions,
and agendas. This is not the Lamb judging humanity. This
is humanity judging the Lamb as being unworthy of their
worship; his redemption is judged to be irrelevant to the
cause of humanity. The horsemen's agendas and actions
are in direct conflict with the purpose and plans of a redeeming Lamb. It is not the Lamb who is destructive; it is
the horsemen who are drunk on their own passions and
desires. Like "children of wrath," they ride pell-mell into
history, trampling underfoot every intention and purpose
of the Lamb.

As John describes the breaking of each seal and the
events that follow, it becomes increasingly evident that the
agenda of the horsemen is diametrically opposed to the

provisions and purposes of the Lamb. Let us briefly note the progression of events outlined by the opening of the seals.

The first horseman breaks forth intent on conquest. However, as has already been noted, there is no recognition of the Lamb or what he provided for humanity. This appears to be a re-enactment of Romans 1:21—*"Although they knew God, they did not glorify Him as God."* Like fools, the horsemen charge forth with their own agenda, which is to go out *"conquering and to conquer"* (Revelation 6:2). The redemptive purpose of the Lamb is cast aside— conquest at any cost is the goal. However, this is conquest outside of any recognition or acknowledgement of the most significant event in history.

The second rider ups the ante to the proverbial "divide and conquer." By taking peace from the earth, the third rider intensifies his plan for conquest by bringing the necessities for life under the control of his barbaric system. When this doesn't achieve the desired goal, the fourth rider takes on God-like power, the power of life and death! However, the power of life and death in the hands of a rider who doesn't even acknowledge the Lamb is despotic power. With the opening of the fifth seal, we come to know just how despotic that thirst for conquest has become.

The opening of the fifth seal reveals *"the souls of those who had been slain for the word of God and for the testimony which they held"* (Revelation 6:9). This obviously indicates that there were still those who worshipped and followed the Lamb. Their allegiance stood opposed to the four horsemen's agenda. Their allegiance was to God and his word. But instead of these faithful ones being welcomed, they become martyrs for not falling in line with the agenda of the horsemen. The fourth horseman transitions into the fifth seal, and when he does so society becomes like a rabid dictatorial leader exercising absolute power by taking the lives of those whose allegiance is to the Lamb. This clearly indicates that the intent of the four riders was to not allow the gospel of the Lamb to disrupt or sidetrack their original plan: world domination, without regard for the Lamb.

The Righteous Revelation of God's Wrath

With the opening of the sixth seal, the stampede of evil is brought face to face with God and the wrath of the Lamb. The redemptive Lamb takes centre stage in the unfolding of Revelation's history. This abrupt change appears to be a fulfillment of Paul's words in Romans 2:5: *"the day of wrath and revelation of the righteous judgment of God."* With the opening of the sixth seal, humanity comes face to face with God and the passionate desire of the Lamb.

Tribulation Theology would have us believe that the Lamb's wrath points to a militaristic ram taking vengeance on those who have ignored him. However, that is allowing the word wrath, as we know and have experienced it in this world, to define the Lamb, rather than allowing the Lamb as the redeemer to define the word wrath.

Let us examine the details of the opening of the sixth seal in order to come to a better understanding of the passage.

In the passage cited from Romans 2:5, Paul also speaks of one *"treasuring up for yourself wrath in the day of wrath."* The breaking of the first five seals reveals a society bent on its own lustful passions, driven by the desires of the flesh and mind. The first four horsemen are like children of wrath bent on their passionate desire for conquest. By nature, these children of wrath follow their own agendas and desires. As pointed out by Paul in Romans, it begins with a lack of thankfulness and spirals downward into ever-increasing degenerative behaviour. As we progress through the opening of the seals, the horsemen's self-serving agenda degenerates to the point where in the opening of the fifth seal humanity acts like the Jews described by Paul in 1 Thessalonians 2:15. The horsemen in charge under the first four seals move into ever deeper expressions of their wrath. They have one agenda in mind—fulfilling their own will and desire, which is to conquer. As children of wrath, they give expression to their treasured-up wrath: those who follow the Lamb and pledge allegiance to the word of God must be removed to accomplish their agenda. So as with the Jews of Paul's day, society's treasured-up wrath causes them to try and silence the proclamation of the very gospel which is humanity's only means of salvation.

It is with the opening of the sixth seal that these children of wrath come face to face with God and the wrath of the Lamb. On this day, the Lamb's wrath is pitted against the children of wrath and this confrontation brings about the *"revelation of the righteous judgment of God."* This day of wrath stands in absolute contrast to any and all wrath described by Tribulation Theology.

The Lamb's Wrath Is Redemptive

To begin our examination of the sixth seal passage, we must ask, is the text to be understood as being literal? If so, the opening of the sixth seal spells out the destruction of the world as we know it, which is how Tribulation Theology has portrayed God's wrath in Revelation.

The opening of the sixth seal triggers a great earthquake. This is followed by John telling us that the sun turns black as sackcloth and the moon turns to blood. Some Tribulation Theology preachers have suggested that this would be a natural result arising from the dust cloud generated in the event of a great earthquake. However, Peter clearly associated this kind of phenomenon with the spiritual shift that happened with the birth of the Church at Pentecost (Acts 2:16–21).

In Acts 2:16, Peter states that Pentecost *"is what was spoken by the prophet Joel,"* and he goes on to quote Joel 2:28–32. Peter's words *"this is what,"* followed by his quotation of Joel 2:28–32, indicates that he saw the happenings at Pentecost as a fulfillment of the words of Joel. This, in spite of the fact that some of the phenomena named did not literally happen. This suggests that Peter uses the passage from Joel to describe the events and spiritual significance of Pentecost metaphorically. John picks up the later part of Joel's prophecy and speaks of the sixth seal as *"the sun became black as sackcloth of hair, and the moon became like blood"* (Revelation 6:12, compare with Joel 2:20). Since John uses some of the same words of Joel, as Peter did, it is suggested that like Peter he sees the events of the breaking of the sixth seal as fulfilling those words.[31] So like Peter, John's use of the quote from Joel suggests he is speaking in metaphorical terms.

As we continue to read Revelation 6:13–14, the problem with a literal interpretation becomes even more difficult. In these verses, John speaks of the stars of heaven falling to earth like figs being blown from a tree by a mighty wind. If we conclude this is a reference to a meteorite shower, we have begun to play with both the literal and symbolic meaning of words, as used by John. Revelation 1:20 indicates that the reference to seven stars designates the pastors of the seven churches. On what basis can our exegesis of Revelation ignore this obvious symbolic use of the word "star"?

John adds to this that the sky rolls up like a scroll, an event that is followed by every mountain and island being moved out of its place. Again, taking this literally would indicate geographical changes of cataclysmic proportions. Yet there is no suggestion on John's part that human life is

---

[31] Given this use of the prophetic passage from Joel, it is suggested that Pentecost and the breaking of the sixth seal have common events. This, in turn, implies that Revelation is presenting a historicist eschatology. However, to follow up and expand on that premise is not the purpose of this book.

in danger or on the brink of extinction. In fact, John's description of how humanity responds to the event indicates that not only is life preserved but all the social and economic structures of society are unaffected. Representatives from every socioeconomic level of society are designated as responding to the events of the sixth seal in exactly the same way.

John's description of humanity's response suggests that the events which take place bring society—en masse—to a singular conclusion and action. Each socioeconomic group is said to seek refuge in the epicentre of the cataclysmic event. Instead of fleeing from the mountains that are moved out off their place, humanity flees to the mountains and seeks to hide *"in the caves and in the rocks of the mountains"* (Revelation 6:15). They call on those same mountains and rocks to *"Fall on us and hide us from the face of Him who sits on the throne and from the wrath of the Lamb!"* (Revelation 6:16) Clearly, it is not destruction or death that is feared; it is exposure to the passionate desires—the wrath—of the redemptive Lamb.

Have you ever picked up a rock and watched the little creatures scurry to the next available hiding place? That is the picture here. God moves the mountains which humanity uses as a hiding place. Their status quo is disrupted. The solid, immovable canopy which was above them and gave them a hiding place from God suddenly disappears. Their normal everyday lives of being masters of their own destiny are suddenly ripped from their control. Rocks and mountains that hid them from God's face are suddenly no longer there and they are exposed to a God-like light. God and the Lamb make them aware of a reality that wasn't considered or acknowledged in the opening of all the previous seals.

Man, in his selfish treasured-up wrath, seeks to be hidden from God. The passionate will, purpose, and desire of the Lamb is ignored. Unregenerate humanity seeks to fulfill its own agendas, and when children of wrath seek to fulfill their own agendas it spells tribulation and martyrdom for the saints. We live in that kind of a world today. These children of wrath do not want exposure to the light and love of God, *"because their deeds were evil"* (John 3:19). They fail to realize that Jesus did not come *"into the world to condemn the world, but that the world through Him might be saved"* (John 3:17). You were not created for destruction. God loves you and wants to redeem you from everything that is destructive. God did not appoint you to follow your own evil will and degenerative desires. The world's insistent resistance to God and the Lamb causes God to show his face and the Lamb of redemption to show his passionate desires.

The Lamb's wrath is totally different from the wrath you have experienced on earth. God's anger against sin was revealed in the death of the Lamb. God will not allow that act to go unnoticed or be relegated to the sidelines. God shows up and sweeps aside all of humanity's constructed barriers against his passionate desires expressed in the gospel and through the Lamb.

Unfortunately, Tribulation Theology has equated "God's face" and the "wrath of the Lamb" of Revelation 6 with judgment and punishment of the sinner. So, Revelation is not seen or presented as a message of hope for the sinner. However, Revelation, like every other book of the New Testament, is part of the gospel message. Jesus did not die so that God would have a case against you. Read the scriptures and you will find that God's face is associated with his glory (Genesis 33:18–23). The Psalmist pleads with God not to hide his face from him (Psalms 27:9). God is not glorified by your destruction! You can be assured that when God shows his face he is serious about establishing a relationship with you! How will you respond?

Seeing God and the Lamb's wrath as something to be feared is a mountain that needs to be removed from the field of theology. God is not the thief who steals, kills, and destroys (John 10:10). God's wrath against sin was revealed in Christ Jesus on the cross, and in that event is revealed the most positive motivation for the redemption of humanity. That positive motivation is God's love for you. God's kingdom is not realized by the same methods as the kingdoms of this world. In God's kingdom, it is the redemptive Lamb who rules as King. God does not intend to destroy ungodliness and unrighteousness by destroying the sinner. It is God's intention to overcome ungodliness and unrighteousness through the redemption of sinners.

Imputing God with the same kind of wrath as we experience at the hands of men and Satan is to impute God with evil. God's wrath cannot be defined by how we experience the wrath of this world. The two have nothing in common.

The Lamb is symbolic of redemption. And like God's wrath, the Lamb's wrath is also holy. Wrath speaks of an overwhelming desire and passion, and the Lamb has an overwhelming desire and passion to redeem humanity.

It is not my intention to provide a detailed defence of the historicist view of Revelation. However, consider the following in respect to the opening of the fifth and sixth seals.

Granting that Revelation deals with the Church's on-going history and that the seals cover the past two thousand plus years of the present era, and allowing each seal to be an introduction to 360 years of that history, the opening of the fifth seal would coincide with the beginning of the Reformation in the sixteenth century.[32]

The reformation was marked by the invention of the printing press and the mass production of the Bible. With the Bible becoming readily available in the fifteenth century, a groundswell of spiritual renewal was begun. It was the personal study of the Bible that gave rise to the reestablishment of the priority of God's word in matters of faith and the life of the Church. This, in turn, gave rise to the Church's renewal. However, many who found the truth of scripture and declared their allegiance to the word of God became martyrs during the Reformation. The established religious organizations of the day did not look kindly on these reformers, and so they were met with the ultimate act of resistance: death. With the dawning of the nineteenth century, this Reformation movement gave rise to the great revival movements of the next two centuries.

---

[32] If the reader is interested in the author's basis for this reasoning, request the book *The Tribulation Is Over*, from Millennium Books, Box 27, Niverville, MB, Canada, R0A 1E0, or call 204-388-4265.

The 1800s saw the birth of the YMCA, the Sunday School movement, the abolishment of child labour practices in factories, and the emergence of mountain-moving missionary organizations. The world's people were exposed to the good news of the gospel like never before. It was the revival of the centuries. Many came into the light of this glorious gospel, fulfilling the words of Daniel: *"And the stone that struck the image became a great mountain and filled the whole earth"* (Daniel 2:35). The mountains of humanity's making were being moved out of their place. God was showing his face. The Lamb's passion was being realized.

It is God's intention that the gospel become the Everest of mountains. And for that reason, God will either move or bring down the mountains created by manmade belief systems. Humanity will not be allowed to hide from God. God will move the manmade belief systems out of their place of dominance in society.

But alas, there were and still are many, as John saw in his vision, who call on the mountains of evolution or their humanly-influenced sciences, philosophies, psychologies, and religions to hide them from the face of God and the wrath of the Lamb. What has been your response to the heightened proclamation of the gospel in our time? Are you trying to hide from the passionate desires of the Lamb? Do you call on your sciences, philosophies, or religious belief systems to hide you from the face of God and the passion of the redemptive Lamb? Are you afraid of the light and truth of the gospel? It is God's intention to let you know that he loves you. God does not want you to perish.

In Revelation, John clearly shows us that the establishment of God's kingdom is under the jurisdiction and administrative mandate of the redemptive Lamb. This redemptive Lamb is central to the unfolding of the apocalypse and the establishment of God's kingdom. The kingdom of God unfolds under the governance of a God-ordained Redeemer—not a rabid lion, militaristic ram, or rampaging devil. And ultimately it is the redemptive Lamb who reigns on the throne with God (Revelation 22:1).

The establishment of God's kingdom can only be realized through the work of the redemptive Lamb. Unfortunately, like the Jews of two thousand years ago, a great portion of the Church continues to hold to the religious idea that the Lamb will become a militaristic ram and pour out his anger against sin and the sinner in order to establish his kingdom. However, God's kingdom is not compatible, nor does it have anything in common, with a beast-like system. God will not network with Satan or a beast-like system in order to establish his will on earth. If God did so, his action would cease to be holy. God's holiness is epitomized in the work of the redemptive Lamb. If our theology concerning God or the Lamb's wrath proclaims and promotes anything other than redemption, our theology has departed from the truth and holiness of the gospel.

In Revelation, the word wrath does not define God or the Lamb. It is God's and the Lamb's redemptive passion which define the word wrath. God's wrath was revealed at the cross, and it was revealed from heaven. The Lamb appeased God's wrath against us.

Like God's wrath, the Lamb's wrath comes from a totally different source than any other kind of wrath. God's wrath gave rise to the gospel, the gospel of redemption! The Lamb's and God's wrath are as far removed from common wrath as heaven is from earth. It is time for the Church to proclaim the Lamb's wrath as redemptive, not militaristic. God's kingdom is founded on the gospel of redemption, and that is the gospel which our theology must proclaim. The purpose and goal of God's and the Lamb's wrath is to bring that redemption to fruition in the realization of the Kingdom of God on this earth.

Revelation sets forth how that kingdom is realized and how it unfolds throughout the history of the Church. It is God's passionate desire to bring his kingdom into its fullness on earth, and that is what God's wrath is all about. God's and the Lamb's wrath was revealed in redemption, and the fruition of that wrath can only showcase the glory of that redemption.

CONCLUSION
God's Wrath Is Good News

In Romans 1:17–18, Paul parallels the revelation of God's wrath with the revelation of God's righteousness. Since the revelation of God's righteousness can only be realized in the special revelation of Jesus Christ, proper biblical exegesis demands that this also be true for the revelation of God's wrath.

Since this special revelation of God's wrath originated from heaven, it is placed in a category all its own. God's wrath has nothing in common with Satan's or humanity's wrath. God's wrath cannot be likened or compared to any other wrath.

God's wrath is holy. There is nothing and no one else who could deal with sin and evil like Jesus did and thereby bring God's intentions, purposes, plans, and goals—in short, his kingdom—into reality. Christ's atoning act also reveals the intensity of God's love for humanity. It is this positive motivation of the revelation of God's wrath that is at the heart of the gospel. The negative side of that revelation is beyond our comprehension and understanding. There are no words which could describe the sense of abandonment that Jesus endured on the cross. Yet his experience of that abandonment and his resulting death brings to term the very heart of God's purpose and desire for humanity. Without it, the redemption of the human race could not have happened. Since no one else could provide that redemption, God himself did so. This places the revelation of God's wrath in the category of an unprecedented holy act.

For theology to suggest that humanity is the object of God's anger implies that God's wrath is no longer holy. It suggests that God's wrath is as common as all other types of wrath. However, scripture does not support this theology. It is true that the sinner is referred to as a child of wrath, but the phrases *"children of wrath"* and the parallel *"vessels of wrath"* describe the sinner in an unregenerate state. This unregenerate state is one in which the unregenerate person fulfills the desires of the flesh and mind. Paul uses the phrases *"children of wrath"* and *"vessels of wrath"* as idiomatic phrases that define the individual who displays this selfish behaviour. In its ultimate state, such behaviour leads the individual to fight against the very gospel that can set him or her free.

Since God dedicated himself to the redemption of humanity, he will not easily be turned aside. In the breaking of the seven seals of Revelation 6, we are given a glimpse into how longsuffering and passionate God's wrath is. In spite of humanity's disregard for the Lamb and his provisions, God does not respond in kind. However, God will not allow humanity to hide behind its rebellious structures. It is God's desire to destroy sin by redeeming the sinner. So God shows his face in the redemptive wrath of the Lamb and sweeps aside the mountains and rocks which humanity uses to hide from God. Daniel 2:35 declares, *"And the stone that struck the image became a great mountain and filled the whole earth."* So it will be! God's intention is for the gospel to become the Everest of mountains. Therefore, God will sweep aside all manmade mountainous belief systems.

God's provision of the Lamb allows for the future to be realized. That future is assured in the redemptive passion of the Lamb. Because of the redemptive passion of the Lamb, Paul could present the revelation of God's wrath as one of three pillars upon which the gospel rests. In Revelation, John describes the details of how the Lamb's wrath brings God's wrath to fruition in the realization of the kingdom of God. God's wrath is not realized in the destruction of sinners but in their redemption. Therefore, Paul was absolutely correct in declaring that he was not ashamed of the gospel. The Revelation of God's wrath and the continued manifestations of that wrath will continue to be redemptive. The Church's proclamation of the gospel must therefore echo Paul's words: *"I am not ashamed of the gospel"* because *"the wrath of God is revealed from heaven"* (Romans 1:16, 18).

And that is *Good News!*

AFTERWORD
A God Kind of Transformation

Have the various views of our present day eschatology (doctrine concerning future events) dealt honestly with the text of Revelation, as given by John? Which view of Revelation and God's wrath would John endorse?

Two thousand years after the fact, it appears that Tribulation Theology (the view of my upbringing) has gotten the popular vote in respect to God's wrath in Revelation. However, the key figure in the multimedia drama that John hears and sees is portrayed symbolically. What John hears and is shown transforms the prophetic Messianic Lion from the Old Testament into a merciful, life-giving New Testament Lamb. This Lamb is the keystone of all biblical revelation, and especially of the New Testament gospel. We need to remind ourselves that Revelation is the final book of the New Testament, the final words of the gospel, and therefore it is the final word in regards to good news.

John lived during the transitional period between the Old Testament and the New Testament, so he was most familiar with the Old Testament symbolic Lion. He looked forward to the day when this prophetic Lion would fulfill his role as the Messiah. Like all other Jews of his time, he believed that this Old Testament symbolism was to be fulfilled in a very specific way. That expectation was wrapped up in the words John hears stated as recorded in Revelation 5:5—*"The Lion of the tribe of Judah, the Root of David, has prevailed to open the scroll."*

The words *"has prevailed"* indicates that the *"Lion of the tribe of Judah"* accomplished what he set out to accomplish. Strong's Concordance defines *prevailed* as "to subdue, conquer, overcome, [and] get the victory."[33] These words describe exactly what John and the disciples expected Jesus to do with the Romans who occupied their country. If anyone could conquer and overcome the Romans, it was Jesus, who John understood to be the *"Lion of the tribe of Judah."* But Jesus did not fulfill John's expected eschatology.

Yet the Angel tells John that the Lion *"has prevailed."* Upon hearing these words, what thoughts must have raced through John's mind? I'm sure some of those thoughts were like the beat of a drum: Where? When? How? However, John doesn't tell us about his thoughts or questions; he doesn't include his personal reaction and

---

[33] See Strong's Concordance #3528.

story. Instead John moves on with recording the events and experiences of the multimedia presentation.

When told about the Lion, he states, *"And I looked, and behold"* (Revelation 5:6).

These words indicate that John is fully concentrated and focused on the Lamb, even though the Lamb is surrounded by the throne, four living creatures, and elders (Revelation 5:6). The Lamb is central to the multimedia presentation and is like the proverbial picture—his appearance tells more than a thousand words.

But again, John doesn't tell us what he was personally experiencing or thinking. Or does he?

Let us pretend we are John for a moment. Upon hearing the words of the elder concerning the *"Lion of the tribe of Judah, the Root of David,"* we would have recalled all that we had been taught and believed about this promised Old Testament Lion.

For John, *"the Lion of the Tribe of Judah"* outranked any and all other prophetic figures—man or beast—in the Old Testament. There wasn't one who stood taller, had more power, or was more significant than the Lion. He would not be defeated, nor would he be overcome. The Lion was the one who would overcome! He was the anticipated deliverer! He was God's answer for Israel! He was the Messiah! And in John's time, he was spoken of and known as *Christ,* which is the Greek rendering of "Messiah" (John 1:41).

In his Gospel, John doesn't give us the details of the birth of Jesus like the other Gospel writers did. Instead John speaks of the *"Word [that] was with God, and the Word [that] was God"* (John 1:1). *"And the Word became flesh and dwelt among us, and we beheld His glory, the glory as of the only begotten of the Father"* (John 1:14). John's Gospel indicates that Jesus was God in flesh on this earth.

John became a disciple of Jesus. Toward the close of his Gospel, John states of him, *"And truly Jesus did many other signs in the presence of His disciples, which are not written in this book; but these are written that you may believe that Jesus is the Christ"* (John 20:30–31). So John believed and confessed that Jesus was the Messiah.

Not only did John become a disciple, he became known as the disciple *"whom Jesus loved"* (John 13:23). He, along with Peter and James, were the "inner three" of the twelve disciples (Mark 9:2, 14:33). And like the other disciples, John was prepared to die bringing about the Messiah's purposes for being on earth (Matthew 26:35). This makes me wonder: was John the one who carried that second sword (Luke 22:38)? Was he ready to spring into action along with Peter in the Garden of Gethsemane (Matthew 26:51)?

But after Peter cuts off Malchus' ear, Jesus tells Peter, *"Put your sword into the sheath. Shall I not drink the cup which My Father has given Me?"* (John 18:11)

Those were disturbing words for John. And added to those words, Jesus allowed himself to be arrested. This was not how the Lion of the tribe of Judah was to act (Matthew 16:21–23). John's eschatology was in question, and it totally disarmed him.

Is it any wonder that we are told that the disciples *"forsook Him and fled"* (Matthew 26:56) when he was arrested?

If he wasn't going to fight for his kingdom to be established, why should they? However, John lets us know that he and Peter followed Jesus to his trial before the high priest (John 18:15). Peter remains outside. John speaks to a servant girl who brings Peter inside, and this precipitates Peter's denial of knowing Jesus (John 18:16).

John's detailed record of the denial may be John's identification with Peter, and the confusion that swirled around in both of their minds. Did either of them know this man? Both he and Peter strongly believed him to be the Messiah, the Saviour of Israel (John 6:68–69), yet he wasn't doing what they expected the Messiah to do. Wasn't he the Lion of the tribe of Judah? Why didn't he allow them to fight? With him as their leader, they would have been victorious. Why did he allow himself to be arrested? This wasn't the script of John's eschatology. This wasn't how they had envisioned the kingdom of God to come into being. This wasn't what was supposed to happen!

John watched the trial and the crucifixion. Then, like a last will and testament, Jesus assigns John the care of his mother, with the words *"Behold your mother"* (John 19:27).

John might have wondered, *Why?* This could only mean that Jesus wouldn't be around to look after his mother, Mary. But Jesus had been like a Lion in the miracles he performed. And like a lion, he vanished into the crowd on many occasions when the people tried to kill him. John must have wondered, *Why is he so impotent? Why does he allow them to crucify him?*

And then he dies!

What is happening? John wondered. *How can the son of God die? He sure isn't like King David! David established the kingdom through destroying the enemy. He sure isn't acting like a lion!*

After Jesus was resurrected, he completed the act of totally crushing and shattering John's eschatological Messianic expectations. Jesus very pointedly told John and the disciples that they would not see the restoration of Israel as a nation (Acts 1:7). John's eschatological expectations became like all ordinary wheat harvest chaff—blown away and scattered by the wind. He is left to wonder, ponder, and surmise about Jesus as the king of a kingdom. When and how would he accomplish what the Lion of the tribe of Judah was expected to accomplish?

With the passing of many years, John becomes an aged preacher. Somehow he picked up the pieces of his experience and proclaims Jesus to be *"the Lamb of God who takes away the sin of the world!"* (John 1:29) And because he didn't stop talking about this Jesus, he is exiled by the Romans to the Island of Patmos (Revelation 1:9). It is here where God arrests him with a reminder of his younger years and reignites his expectations concerning the Lion of the tribe of Judah.

In his virtual reality experience, he turns to see the *"Lion of the tribe of Judah."* He is both shocked and thrilled by what he sees: a precious Lamb! Not simply the lamb that John the Baptist said would take away the sin of the world, but a precious, endearing Lamb—the Lamb that he had a very deep emotional attachment to, as deep an attachment as Jesus had to him. John had preached about this Lamb his whole life. In fact, this Lamb *was* his life. This Lamb had turned his world upside-down. He had thought that Rome was his personal enemy. In his younger years, he had thought they were God's enemy, too. But the Lamb had transformed all those beliefs. This Lamb suffered an intentional, barbaric death on a Roman cross. But on the third day he came back to life. Jesus' death and resurrection gave John freedom from the condemnation of sin, a freedom that was more real than being freed from the Romans. The veil of the temple, which had constantly reminded him that he could not have an audience with God as father, had been *"torn in two from top to bottom"* (Matthew 27:51).

In his youth, John had constantly been reminded of his and Israel's shortcomings. Every year, they would offer a lamb for sin, but this annual tradition only became a constant reminder that righteousness was unattainable. He never felt God was as close as a father. However, his precious Lamb had transformed him and his story! In Jesus Christ, as the precious Lamb, he had come to know God as a *loving Father!* His world had totally changed! He no longer saw Rome as the enemy, even though it was the Romans who had exiled him to Patmos. He was willing to die for this Lamb. All of Rome's legions couldn't stop him from following the Lamb.

Because of the endearing Lamb, he had fellowship and communion with God beyond the comprehension of the mind (Revelation 1:10). He had access to the very presence of God, and he had found him to be a true Father—a father like Jesus had described him to be. He wanted the

Romans to have that same communion with God as their Father.

John believed God wanted Jews and Gentiles to be one in the kingdom of God! In his youth, that had been unthinkable. But not anymore! Now it was a living reality. So, like Paul, he had gone to preach to the Gentiles. And that was the reason he was on the Island of Patmos.

His experiences with God and the gospel had taught him that Jesus had come to bring freedom and peace to the world. God loved the Romans as much as he loved John. God wanted to make the Romans, and all people, just as much a part of the kingdom as Israel. So Jesus had come to accomplish his father's desire. It wasn't Rome that Jesus saw as the enemy; it was sin and Satan. God wanted the Romans to have life in Jesus, and so did John. He wanted all people to appreciate and follow the Lamb like he did.

So for John, the Lamb he sees is precious because that Lamb represents a life that had been unavailable to his forefathers, and to the world. Because of that Lamb, the Romans weren't God's enemy and neither were they John's enemy. The magnitude of what he sees totally overwhelms him—the Lion of the tribe of Judah transformed into a Lamb! What a concept!

His realization of the depth of meaning in what he sees is heady. Love the world so much that you die for it. Overcome sin, death, and the devil by dying for sinners. Incredible! This is definitely not society's kind of thinking or action.

For the Lion to become a Lamb... that is a God kind of transformation.

And what John saw transformed his eschatology! The Lamb pointed the way to the future.

Does the world need to be delivered from evil? Yes, it does! Who will do it? How will it happen? Will it be done by a lion or a ram-like warrior? Will it be through untold suffering and destruction, or will it be done through a God kind of transformation?

John saw a Lamb. For John, this Lamb was precious. This Lamb had transformed his life, and was transforming his world. Without the Lamb, there was no future!

Have you allowed the Lamb of God, Jesus Christ, to transform your life, your world, and your future?

He can, he will, and he is waiting to do so for you!

—H. DAVE DERKSON
Abbotsford B.C.
August 2010

BIBLIOGRAPHY

Barth, Marcus. *Ephesians 1–3: The Anchor Bible* (Garden City, NY: Doubleday & Company, Inc.), 1974.

Cranfield, C.E.B. *Romans: A Shorter Commentary* (Grand Rapids, MI: Wm. Eerdmans), 1985.

Daube, David, *The New Testament and Rabbinic Judaism* (Peabody, MA: Henderickson Publishers Inc.). Reprinted by arrangement with the School of Oriental and African Studies, University of London, 1956.

Dodd, C. H. *The Epistle of Paul to the Romans.* (London, UK: The Moffat New Testament Commentary, Hodder and Stuaghton), 1932.

Lloyd-Jones, Dr. Martyn. *Romans: The Gospel of God, An Exposition of Chapter 1.* (Grand Rapids, MI: Ministry Resources Library, Zondervan), 1991.

Manning, Brennan. *The Ragamuffin Gospel.* (Sisters, OR: Multnomah Books), 1990.

Morris, Leon. *The Epistle to the Romans* (Grand Rapids, MI: Wm. Eerdmans), 1988.

Osborne, Grant R. *Revelation: Baker Exegetical Commentary on the New Testament* (Grand Rapids, MI: Baker Academic), 2002.

Kittel, Gerhard, Ed. *Theological Dictionary of the New Testament* (Grand Rapids, MI: Wm. Eerdmans), 1977. Volumes 1–10.

Strong's Exhaustive Concordance. (Nashville, TN: Crusade Bible Publishers, Inc.), n.d.